Papst Clemens

Interesting Letters Of Pope Clement 14

Vol. II

Papst Clemens

Interesting Letters Of Pope Clement 14
Vol. II

ISBN/EAN: 9783743356092

Manufactured in Europe, USA, Canada, Australia, Japa

Cover: Foto ©ninafisch / pixelio.de

Manufactured and distributed by brebook publishing software (www.brebook.com)

Papst Clemens

Interesting Letters Of Pope Clement 14

INTERESTING LETTERS

OF
POPE CLEMENT XIV.
(GANGANELLI.)

TO WHICH ARE PREFIXED,

ANECDOTES OF HIS LIFE.

TRANSLATED FROM THE FRENCH EDITION PUB-
LISHED AT PARIS BY LOTTIN LE JEUNE.

THE FIFTH EDITION.
VOL. II.

LONDON:
PRINTED FOR R. BALDWIN, IN PATER-NOSTER ROW; AND
T. BECKET IN THE STRAND.
M DCC LXXXI.

EXPLANATION

OF THE

VIGNETTE,

IN THE

TITLE-PAGE OF THIS VOLUME.

THE Vignette reprefents a Woman fitting upon Clouds fupported by the Efcutcheon of POPE GANGANELLI's Arms: She difplays the Symbols of thofe Virtues by which CLEMENT XIV. was characterifed —Fortitude, Temperance, Prudence, and Vigilance, are indicated by a Column, a Bit, a Bridle, a Mirror, and a Cock: The Olive-branch is the fymbol of his Character, as a Maker of peace, and the Palm denotes the fuccefs of his enterprifes. Near him is a Pyramid, erected to the Glory of GANGANELLI:—Below we fee the Efcutcheons of *France, Spain, Naples,* and *Portugal,* united with that of the *Pope*; the bundle of Faggots is the Symbol of the concord of thofe Powers. Above we fee iffuing from behind the Clouds, a body of Rays which illuminate the Virtues and form the Glory of his Holinefs.

LETTERS, &c.

LETTER LXXV.

TO THE PRELATE CERATI.

IF this letter was to carry all my sentiment, you would not find it a light one; for I would load it with all the esteem, all the attachment, and all the admiration I am capable of, to convince you, more than ever, how much I revere, and how much I love you.

I have seen the Augustine Monk whom you recommended to me, and have found him, as you told me, full of the Fathers of the Church. They are upon his lips, they are in his heart, and he is the man in the world that we can perufe with the greateſt pleafure, when his full value is known. His hero is, with reafon, St. Auguſtine, becaufe he was an univerfal Teacher, embracing all Science, and was fingularly favoured by it. Excellent encomiums have been made upon that incomparable man: but he has not been praifed as he deferves. Some time ago I advifed an Ecclefiaſtick who confulted me about compofing a panegyrick on that great Saint, to fay nothing of his own, but to extract all from the holy Father's writings, thinking that Auguſtine himfelf only was capable of praifing St. Auguſtine worthily. He has followed my advice; and we have feen the moſt fublime and affecting paffages of this great Teacher compofe his eulogium. It was extremely well connected, though here and there interrupted with exclamations and ejaculations, which affected the Audience. When will our Rhetoricians and our Preachers know, that true eloquence

quence does not confift either in being witty or elegant; but in an expreffion of the foul, an ebullition of the heart, which burns, aftonifhes, and works wonders?

There are certain moments where the great Orators feem neither to have ftyle nor words, left the fublimity fhould be degraded by ftudied phrafes.

There are people who put themfelves into an *alembic* to be eloquent, and nothing iffues from that operation but forced conceits and bombaft phrafes; whereas, if they would give themfelves up to the energy of their hearts, they would have golden tongues.

I find nothing but elegance in almoft all the writings of the times, and yet they are very far from being eloquent. Elegance pleafes, but eloquence captivates; and when it is natural, it *amalgamates* itfelf with all the beauties of nature and genius, to fhow them in all their luftre, and according to truth—it is, in a word, fuch as that part of your compofition which you fhowed me fome time ago, where I could fee the true touch of Demofthenes, notwithftanding the immenfe interval which has paffed from his time to your's.

Nothing is more admirable than to approach to the Ancients, and, notwithftanding the diftance of time, to adhere ftrongly to them, as if you were their cotemporary; for it muft be confeffed, that they have reaped all, and we come only to glean.

I was requefted fome time ago to compofe a Scientifick Difcourfe, which was to be placed at the head of a book of Geometry. I collected my whole force, and in the ebullition of a work which lafted more than a week, I thought I had produced fomething very interefting and quite new; but I cannot tell you how I was furprifed and humbled to find all my thoughts fcattered over a few pages of the Ancients. In the mean time I was no plagiary; but the mind of man having only one circle, all generations nearly refemble each other in their manner of thinking, although the tints may confiderably differ.

I have

I have lately had a perfon of the name of Sagri prefented to me, juft come from the Schools of Pifa—he appears to have wherewithal to make a confiderable figure. But into what hands will he fall ? The moment a young man leaves College is the inftant which decides his fate; and all either proves abortive, or all produces good fruit. I have feen fome who gained all the prizes, and have been mentioned with honour as true Coriphæus's; yet, notwithftanding all this emphatic admiration, have become lefs than nothing. They have been entangled by criminal pleafures, or engaged in mechanical employments; or their talents, after having made an effort, were exhaufted by the laborious operation, and could produce nothing more. They are like to early fruit, which charms by the gaiety of the colours and the novelty, but is blighted at the moment you admire, and are difpofed to gather it.

What a deal of trouble before the mind arrives at perfection! All that I know is, that mine thinks it has gained it, when it

B 3   fhares

shares with your's by a communication of ideas, and puts me in a situation to repeat my sentiments of attachment and respect, &c.

ROME, 15th Aug. 1754.

LETTER LXXVI.

TO CARDINAL QUIRINI.

MOST EMINENT,

THE different reflections which your Eminency has made upon the different Ages that have passed from the beginning of the world, are worthy of such a genius as your's. I think I see Reason weighing all these Ages, some like ingots, others like leaves of tinsel. In fact, there are some so solid, and others so light, that they make the most astonishing contrast.

Our's, without contradiction, is more marked than any other by its lightness; but

but it pleafes, it feduces, efpecially by the good offices of the French, who have given it an elegance, which, in fpite of us we find agreeable.

The Ancients would have murmured, and with reafon; yet if they had lived in our times, they would have fuffered themfelves to be led away as we are, and been as well amufed with our trifling difcourfe and airy writings.

The ancient Roman tafte and correctnefs might not perhaps have relifhed fuch flight compofitions; but the Romans of thefe days are not fo nice as formerly. French elegance has paffed the Alps, and we have received it with complacency, at the very moment we were criticifing it.

Your Eminency, who loves the French, has certainly looked with a forgiving eye upon their *prettinefs*, though it might have offended the fuperior tafte of the ancient manners. There is no evil but may be found collectively in all ages; there are fparks and flames, lilies and bluebottles, rains and dews, ftars and meteors, rivers and rivulets, which is a perfect picture of nature; and to judge of the world and of times, you muft unite the different views, and make but one piece of the whole.

The Ages do not all refemble one another; it is their variety which helps us to judge; without this difference there would be no comparing. I know we fhould prefer living in an Age which prefented nothing to the view but what was great; but we muft take the times as they come, and not continually regret the paft, to tie ourfelves to the chariot-wheels of the Ancients. Let us endeavour to preferve their tafte, and we fhall have nothing to fear from our own utility.

We cannot look without horrour upon the gulf from whence the Ages iffue, and into which they are precipitating. What a number of years, months, days, hours minutes, and feconds, are abforbed by eternity, which is always the fame, and remains immoveable in the midft of change and revolutions! It is a rock in the midft of the fea, againft which the waves beat in vain. We are but like grains of fand, with
which

which the wind fporteth, if we do not attach ourfelves immoveably to that point of fupport. It is there your Eminency hath caft anchor; it is that which has made you undertake fo many learned writings which all Europe admires, and Religion applauds.

I never am tired with reading the account of your travels, efpecially the defcriptions you have given of Paris and France. Befides that the Latin may be compared with that of St. Jerome, there are admirable reflections on every thing which your Eminency has met with. What a penetrating eye is your's? It fearches the effence of things, the fubftance of writings, and the fouls of the writers. You have had the happinefs to fee feveral great men at Paris who are ftill alive, the precious remains of the Age of Louis XIV. and who muft have convinced you, that that Age has not been exalted beyond its merit.

Nothing opens the mind fo much as Travels; I read them as much as I can, that I may make my thoughts range, though my body is fedentary. What I am certain of is, that I am often in idea at Brefcia;

Brescia; that town which your Lordship enriches by your example and precepts, and where you hourly receive homage; to which I unite, with all my soul, the profound respect with which I am, &c.

ROME, 10th Dec. 1754.

LETTER LXXVII.

TO CARDINAL BANCHIERI.

MOST EMINENT,

I HAVE not yet seen the person from Ferrara, whom your Eminency deigned to recommend to me; but I have nevertheless announced him to the Keeper of the *Ara Cœli*, who will do every thing in his power to prove to you how much the interest you seem to have in this Person is dear to him.

I wish my employment would allow me to take a journey to Ferrara; that town so celebrated for many events, and which

which has the happiness to possess your Eminency, and the ashes of Ariosto. My first care would be to go and visit them. Some poetick sparks would issue forth, enflame me, and enable me to assure you in verse, as well as in prose, that nothing can equal the profound respect with which I am, &c.

Rome, 7th Jan. 1754.

LETTER LXXVIII.

TO A CANON OF MILAN.

SIR,

A PANEGYRICK on Saint Paul is no small undertaking. It requires a soul equal to the Teacher of the Gentiles, to celebrate him in the manner he deserves. His eulogium is the eulogium of Religion; they are so essentially united that they cannot be praised separately.

You find in this great Apostle the same spirit, the same zeal, and the same charity. How rapid should your pen be, if you would describe his Travels and Apostolical Labours! He flies as swift as thought when he is about to undertake a good work; and breathes nothing but Jesus Christ when he preaches the Gospel. One would believe, by the manner in which he multiplies himself, that he alone formed the whole Apostolical College: he is at the same instant on land and sea, always watching for the salvation of the Faithful, always desiring the palm of martyrdom, always pressing forward to eternity. Nobody was so good a citizen, so good a friend; he forgot nothing; he remembered the smallest services that were done him; and his heart did not once palpitate, but with a desire for Heaven, which enlightened him; or with a movement of love for Jesus Christ, who converted him; or with an act of acknowledgment to those Christians who assisted him.

Panegyrick, in general, is a kind of writing which should not resemble a sermon; it should lighten, but the flashes should burst from a fund of morality, which ought

ought to be the basis of the Discourse. They do not instruct who only praise; and they do not celebrate their Hero, who confine themselves solely to instruct.

The skill of the Orator consists in producing from the bosom of the eulogium shining reflections, which should have in view the reformation of morals. But above all things, my dear Friend, take care that you do not make a panegyrick for one Saint at the expence of another; nothing can better prove the sterility of the Orator. Every illustrious person has his merit, and it is an insult to the memory of one servant of God, who looked upon himself as the lowest of all, to raise his glory to the prejudice of another.

Let there be no digressions foreign from your subject. Do not forget that it is St. Paul whom you mean to praise; and that you miss your aim, if you attach yourself to any thing but his eulogium.

No languors are to be excused in panegyrick—all ought to be rapid, and especially in that of the great Apostle, whose zeal was always active. Your audience
should

should believe they see and hear him, that they may say, "It is he, behold him!" You should, like him, display all the powers of grace; like him discomfit all those who would lessen the absolute dominion of God over the heart of man; and like him, thunder against the false Prophets, and the corrupters of morals. And in the end, you should give a succinct account of his different Epistles, and present them burning with the flames of Charity, and radiating with the lights of Truth.

No forced comparisons should here have place; they ought to rise out of the subject—no useless words be admitted; every sentence should be instructive:—no bombast phrases; they ought to be all natural. Your heart, and not your imagination, should be the Orator in this Discourse. Reserve your rhetorical flights for the Academies, when you are to pronounce an Eulogium there; but the dignity of the pulpit, the sanctity of the Temple, the eminence of the subject, in fine the Panegyrick of Paul, are all superior to Antitheses.

Human

Human eloquence is intended to praise human actions; but divine eloquence is requisite to celebrate divine men. It is not among the Poets that you should gather flowers to crown the Elect, but from among the Prophets. I am more than I can tell, &c.

Rome, 30th Oct. 1755.

LETTER LXV.

TO THE ABBE LAMI.

I CANNOT join in your opinion, my dear Abbé, of the book you have criticised with so much severity. I do not think so indifferently of it as you do. It contains principles, views, and beauties, which render it interesting. Some negligences of style do not entirely disfigure a book. The stile is only the bark; and sometimes the tree may be good, though the bark is good for nothing. Unfortunately in this age we are less attached to things

things than to words. The diction too often determines the fate of a book. I have ran over a multitude of Pamphlets printed at Paris, which had nothing in them but a rapid and seducing style. A man is obliged to ask, himself what the author meant to say, and yet he does not know. It is not surprising, that in a country where they are so singularly fond of dress and tinsel, they should be pleased with a production, whose outward appearance constitutes all its merit.

There are some subjects that of themselves are sufficient to captivate the attention; while there are others which will not be regarded, without the passport of a brilliant style. An able Writer should attend to this difference.

I shall be very glad if you will analyse two different works which have just appeared here; *Conversation with one's-self* and *The Elements of Metaphysicks*. The first is singularly interesting, as it elevates the soul upon the wreck of the passions and senses. The second is not less so, as it tends to render its spirituality and immortality

tality demonftrable. Thefe are two metahyfical productions differently prefented: the *Converfation* with a clearnefs which makes it univerfally underftood; the *Elements* with a depth which prevents its being generally read.

I look upon your Papers as an alarumbell, which prevents our Italians from fleeping over Literature and the Sciences. In a warm climate there is need of being frequently roufed, in order to ftudy. The mind flumbers like the body, if we do not take care to fpur it up; and in that ftate we have neither fpirit to read nor to think.

Florence was always renowned for learning and tafte, and I am not afraid of the Florentines degenerating while you continue to inftruct them. A periodical work executed with difcernment, gives light to the underftanding, fupports emulation, and makes up for the want of perufing a multitude of works, which we have not time to read, or means to procure.

When I read a Journal which gives an account of the productions printed in Europe,

rope, I learn to know the genius of the different nations; and I perceive that an Englishman, does not write like a German, nor think like a Frenchman. This national difference, which diftinguifhes the people by their manner of writing and thinking, perfuades me that the moral world is a copy of the natural one, and that there are minds like faces, which have no fort of refemblance.

Adieu! I leave you to throw myfelf among the thorns of controverfy, where I certainly fhall not find the flowers which I perceive in your writings.

ROME, 5th Nov. 1755.

LETTER LXXX.

TO A CURATE OF THE DIOCESE OF RIMINI.

IT is with great rashness, my dear Pastor, that you judge your father, mine, the Father of all the Faithful, the great Lambertini, for whom all the Churches have the greatest veneration. Besides his being celebrated for his extensive and sublime knowledge, for his penetrating genius, for his consummate prudence; he is the chief of our Religion, the Sovereign Pontiff, of whom we cannot speak any ill without blasphemy. You are not ignorant of St. Paul's having begged pardon of the High-Priest of the Synagogue, although it was expiring, because he had called him a *whited wall.*

The treaty which Benedict XIV. made with Spain, that the Spanish Clerks should come no more to Rome, has prevented, I do not know how many young Ecclesiasticks from being vagabonds, and leading licentious lives. Nothing is more proper than

than to see those who are destined for the Ministry studying under the eyes of their own Bishops, who learn to know them, and do not lose sight of them.

Besides there are so many reasons required for judging a Sovereign with equity, that if we do not know what passes in the Cabinet of Princes, the nature of events, the consequences which an affair may have; and if even we cannot penetrate the souls of those who act themselves, or employ others to do so, we cannot form any judgement but an unjust one.

Alas!—who are we who condemn the Vicar of Christ; and, above all, while we are ignorant of the motives of his proceedings, or without knowing what he could foresee? In every kind of business, prejudice should be in favour of the Judge. How can they be justified who take the liberty, on slight appearances, to blame the conduct of the Sovereign Pontiff? This is undoubtedly giving arms to the Protestants, and failing essentially in the respect that is due to him whom God has established upon a throne to see and

to

to judge; and to whom he hath ordained that we fhould hearken as to himfelf—I fay more. it is to rifk falvation.

There is not a circumftance, nor a moment, that our hearts or opinions fhould be capable of rifing up againſt the proceedings of the Sovereign Pontiff, unlefs we are of his Council. He fees what you cannot fee, and if he does not account to us, it is becaufe he is bound by confiderations which withhold both his tongue and his pen. There is a Chriftian policy, which, without injuring truth, does not declare the whole of it: and which envelopes itfelf in a prudent referve, when it is proper to keep filence. How can you preach to your parifhioners the refpect due to the Head of the Church, if they hear you yourfelf declaim againſt him? Suppofe even that he has done amifs, you ought, as a Chriftian, as a Prieſt, as a Paftor, to excufe him in Publick, and impofe an eternal filence on thofe who would dare to attack him. Thefe are my fentiments with regard to Sovereign Pontiffs. They are the Annointed of the Lord, the Chriſts of whom

whom we never should speak ill: *Nolite tangere Christos meos, & in Prophetis meis malignari* *.

I flatter myself that you will get the better of this prejudice, and that you will approve my reasons, because you have a reasonable mind and a good heart. It is an effervescence of the imagination which led you to condemn Benedict XIV. whose proceedings are weighed in the scales of justice, and even in the sanctuary of truth. I embrace you, my dear Pastor, and am, &c.

Rome, 14th May, 1755.

* Touch not mine Anointed, and do my Prophets no harm.

LETTER LXXXI.

TO MR. MEKNER, A PROTESTANT GEN-
TLEMAN.

I AM forry, my dear Sir, to hear you perpetually repeating a multitude of objections which have been employed againſt the Church of Rome, and which M. Boſſuet, a French Biſhop, has demoliſhed in his expoſition of the Catholick Faith, and in his excellent work on the Diverſity of Opinions. It is impoſſible to follow the track of a Proteſtant, becauſe inſtead of waiting an anſwer to his queſtion he propoſes a new one, and never gives time to breathe.

If you ſpeak to me all at once of Purgatory, the Euchariſt, and the worſhip of Saints, it is impoſſible for me to reply to three points at one inſtant. If we would underſtand a controverſy, it ſhould be carried on in a rational manner; and, conſequently, it is neceſſary that one ſubject

ject be examined to the bottom before you pafs to another. Without that we beat the air, and fhall have the fate of all wranglers, who after long difputation, go off, each obftinate in his original opinion.

You are fatisfied with the plan I have laid down to prove by the Gofpel, and by the Epiftles of St. Paul, which you receive as infpired works, all the truths which you conteft; and to fhow you that uninterrupted tradition hath always taught them.

If it was otherwife, you fhould know the day and the date when we made the innovation; at leaft, if you would not perfuade us that the whole Church, in the twinkling of an eye, notwithftanding its members are difperfed all over the world, did change its belief without perceiving it. What an abfurdity!

The reproaches which you are conftantly making againft the Romifh Church, my dear Sir, on the celibacy prefcribed to the Priefts, and on the cup which is withheld from the Faithful in partaking of the holy myfteries, fall of themfelves when we think that marriage and the priefthood are united daily among the Greek Catholicks: and there alfo they gave the Faithful the Communion in both kinds.

Return to the Church with fincerity, and the Pope who governs at prefent will not throw you from his bofom, becaufe you have Minifters who are married, and becaufe you defire the ufe of the cup. His prudence will find a modification, which will grant you all that he can grant, without altering opinions and morals, but only changing the difcipline, which has at all times varied.

Cardinal Quirini, whofe zeal for your return confumes him, will be your mediator with the Holy Father. In returning to the Pope you will return to him who was formerly your Chief, for it is you who have withdrawn. The abufes which reigned at that time in the Church, *becaufe it is neceffary*, as Jefus Chrift faid, *that there be offences and herefies*, cannot abfolutely authorife our anceftors, in revolting and feparating themfelves. They had no other method but that of remonstrating; and if they had stopped there, without mixing either sourness, gall, or a spirit of rebellion, they would certainly have obtained some reform. To heal some tumors in the body, we neither think of mutilating or smothering it.

Many Protestants would return, if they were not withheld by wretched worldly reasons; for it is impossible but in reading the Holy Scriptures so often as they do, they must perceive the prerogatives of the Chief of the Apostles, and the infallibility of the Church, which can never teach any error; and the more so, as Christ is truely with Her, even to the consummation of time, without interruption: *Omnibus diebus vitæ, usque ad consummationem sæculi.*

There need but eyes to see whether the Romish or the Protestant Church is right. The one appears to be that Holy Mountain of which the scripture speaks; and the other, a vapour which dims the sight, and has no solidity.

I would

I would give the laft drop of my blood, my dear Sir, to fee you all reunited to us again, being certain that you have broken the chain which tied you to the centre of unity, and that you are no longer but folitary beings, without compafs, guide, or chief.

God makes you feel it in the moft terrible manner, in giving you up to I don't know how many errors, which form almoft as many different fects as there are communions: and that circumftance proves to us, that fince there is no longer an authority to unite the Faithful, they truft to their own judgements, and are led away by prejudice.

Do not imagine that I mean to infult your fituation. Alas! every thing tells me that you have the good faith; but that will not juftify you before God, who requires a ftrict examination upon fo effential an article; and the more fo, as no one is more capable of judging than you are yourfelf.

The fentence which a man pronounces againft himfelf, when in the wrong is the

beft

best reproof, and is worthy of your candid soul and good heart. Your candour promises me, that you will inform yourself of the truth, and will not reject it when you see it. It is upon the lips of good Catholicks, and in hearing them you hear it. I desire it in all the fullness of my heart, by the sincere ardour I have to find myself with you in the Dwelling of Peace, where there will be only those who are marked with the sign of the Faith. Judge by that of the extensive attachment with which I have the honour to be, &c.

Rome, 14th May, 1753.

LETTER LXXXII.
TO PRINCE SAN-SEVERO.

THE petrefactions I have sent you are not worth your thanks. I know the value, as well as the advantage, of entering into a correspondence with a Philosopher who is occupied in studying the history of Nature, and who does not admire her sports and phenomena, but with a knowledge of their cause.

The

The birds you are importing from the New World for the Emperour, are extremely curious; but, notwithſtanding every precaution, I doubt of their getting to our climate alive. People have frequently tried to bring over different kinds of humming-birds, but always have had the mortification of ſeeing them die at ſome diſtance from our coaſts.

Providence, by giving us the Peacock, has provided us moſt richly, without our going in ſearch of winged beauties elſewhere. In reality, America has nothing more beautiful than our own birds; but we commonly prefer what is foreign, becauſe it comes from a diſtance.

You will be enchanted, my Lord, with the undertaking of Monſ. de Buffon, the French Academician, and with the volumes of that Author which have appeared. I know them only by the extracts that have been given from them, and they appear admirable. Yet I am ſorry that the Author of a Natural Hiſtory ſhould declare for a ſyſtem: It muſt be a means of having many things which he advances doubted, and oblige him to combat all those who are not of his opinion. Besides, where he wanders from the book of Genesis on the creation of the world, he has no support but paradoxes, or, at best, hypotheses.

Moses, as an inspired Author, is the only one who could instruct us in the formation and unfolding of the world. He is not an Epicurus, who has recourse to atoms; a Lucretius, who believes matter to be eternal; a Spinosa, who admits a material God; a Descartes, who prates about the laws of motion; but a Legislator, who announces to all men without hesitation, without fear of being mistaken, how the world was created. Nothing can be more simple or more sublime than his opening: *In the beginning God created the Heaven and the Earth.* He could not speak more assuredly if he had been a spectator; and by these words, mythology, systems, and absurdities shrink to nothing, and become mere chimeras in the eyes of reason.

The man who does not perceive the truth in the relation of Moses was not formed for the knowledge of it. Some people

people are conftantly attached to hypo-
thefes, without even the leaft probability,
and yet are unwilling to believe what
gives the higheft idea of the power and
wifdom of God.

An eternal world offers a thoufand
greater difficulties, than an eternal intelligence; and a co-eternal world is an abfurdity which cannot exift, becaufe nothing
can be fo ancient as God himfelf. Not to
mention that he is neceffary, and that
the world is not neceffary; from what
right fhall matter, a thing whofe exiftence
is entirely contingent, whofe nature is abfolutely inert, pretend to the fame prerogatives with an all-powerful and immaterial fpirit? Thefe are extravagancies
which could only be produced by a di-
ftracted imagination, and prove the aftonifhing weaknefs of man when he will only
hearken to himfelf.

The hiftory of Nature is a book fhut for
all generations, if we do not perceive the
exiftence of God, and his being a creator
and preferver; for nothing can be more
evident than his action. The Sun, all-mag-
nificent

nificent as he is, although adored by different nations, has neither intelligence nor difcernment; and if his courfe is fo regular as never to be even for a moment interrupted, it is through the impulfe received from a Supreme agent, whofe orders he executes with the greateft punctuality.

Wherever we caft our eyes over the vaft extent of the univerfe, we fee the immenfity of a Being, before whom this world is as nothing, when the fmalleft work cannot exift without a Maker; it would be very extraordinary, if this world could have the privilege of owing its exiftence and its beauty to itfelf alone. Reafon digs frightful precipices for itfelf, when it hearkens only to the paffions and fenfes: and reafon without faith is to be pitied. All the academies of the univerfe may fancy fyftems on the creation of the world; but after all their refearches, all their conjectures, all their combinations, the multitudes of volumes, they will tell me much lefs than Mofes has told me in a fingle page; and will tell me things too, that are entirely deftitute of probability. Such

is the difference between the man who
speaks only from himself, and the man
who is inspired.

The Eternal smiles from on high at all
these mad systems which fancifully arrange the world; sometimes giving chance
for its parent, and sometimes supposing it
to exist from eternity.

Some people love to persuade themselves
that matter governs itself, and that there is
no other deity; because they well know
that matter is stupid and inactive, and
therefore need not dread its effects; while
the justice of a God, who sees every thing,
and weighs every thing, is dreadful to the
sinner.

Nothing can be more beautiful than the
history of Nature, when it is united to that
of Religion. Nature is nothing without
God; it produces every thing, vivifies
every thing by his help. Without being
any part of what composes the universe,
he is the movement, the sap, and the life
of it. Let his activity cease, there will be
no more activity in the elements, no more
vegetation in plants, no more spring in second

cond caufes, no more revolutions of the ftars. Eternal darknefs muft take place of light, and the univerfe become its own grave.

The fame thing would happen to this world, were God Almighty to withdraw his hand, which happens to our bodies when all motion ceafes. They fall into duft, they are exhaled in fmoke, and it is not even known that they ever exifted.

If I had fufficient knowledge to undertake a hiftory of Nature, I would begin my work by difplaying the immenfe perfections of its Author; then treat of man as his mafter-piece; and fucceffively from fubftance to fubftance, from kind to kind, I would defcend to the fmalleft ant, and fhow in the leaft infect, as well as in the moft perfect angel, the fame wifdom fhining forth, and the fame Almighty hand employed.

A picture of this nature would neceffarily engage the lovers of Truth—and Religion herfelf, by whom the defign was traced out, would render it infinitely precious.

Let us never fpeak of the creatures, except to bring us nearer to our Creator: they

are

are the reverberation of his never-failing light, and thefe are ideas which either raife or debafe us; for man is never more diminutive nor more grand, than when he confiders himfelf in his relation to God. He then perceives an Infinite Being whofe image he is, and before whom he is but as an atom: two apparent contradictions, which muft be reconciled, to give a juft idea of ourfelves, that we may not run into the exceffes of the proud angels, nor into thofe of unbelievers, who level themfelves with the beafts that perifh.

Your Letter, my Lord, led me to thefe reflections; and I confefs to you at the fame time, that I have no greater fatisfaction than when I find an opportunity of fpeaking of the Deity. He is the element of our hearts, and it is only in his love that the foul bloffoms.

Happily, I was fenfible of this great truth in my earlieft years, and in confequence I chofe the Cloifter, as a retreat where, feparated from the creatures, I could commune more eafily with the Creator. The commerce of the world is so turbulent, that while we are in it we scarcely know the recollection necessary to unite us with God.

I thought of writing a Letter, and I have written a Sermon; except that, instead of finishing with *Amen*, I conclude with the respect which is due to you, and with which I have the honour to be, &c.

Rome, 13th December, 1754.

LETTER LXXXIII.

TO COUNT ALGAROTTI.

MY dear Count, it is a long time since I have had the pleasure of conversing with you, or rather, since I was at your school. A little disciple of Scotus cannot do better than profit by the lessons of a Philosopher, who has brought to light the Newtonism of the Ladies.

A system of philosophy founded on attraction ought more particularly to be your's, because you have such an attractive, amiable

amiable character, that you draw all minds after you; but for my part, I would rather, with such advantages, be less a Newtonian, and more a Christian.

We were not created to be either the disciples of Aristotle or Newton. Our souls have a much nobler destiny; and the more your's is sublime, the more you ought to remount to its source.

You may say, as often as you please, that it is the business of a Monk to preach; and I will repeat to you continually, that it is the business of a Philosopher to employ himself in thinking from whence he came, and whither he goes. We have all a cause, and final purpose for our existence, and it must be God alone who is both the one and the other.

Your philosophy, notwithstanding your reasonings, rests only upon chimeras, if you separate it from Religion. Christianity is the substance of the truths which man ought to seek after: but he loves to nurse himself in error, as the reptiles love to satiate themselves on the mud in the ditch. We seek at a distance what we may find in ourselves,

selves, would we only look within, as did the great St. Auguftine; who having taken a view of every being, to fee if he could find his God, returned to his own heart, and declared that he exifted more there than any where elfe—*Et redii ad me.*

I hope you will preach to me one day, and that each of us fhall have his turn. Ah! I wifh to God!—However, whether you moralife or banter, I will always hear you with that pleafure which one muft have in hearing thofe they cordially love, and to whom they are from inclination as well as duty, the moft humble, &c.

Rome, 7th December, 1754.

LETTER LXXXIV.
TO THE ABBE PAPI.

BEHOLD, my dear Abbé, the learned Cardinal Quirini is juſt gone to unite his knowledge to God, and to take full draughts from that torrent of light, which we cannot perceive here below, but through clouds. He died as he lived, with his pen in his hand, finiſhing a line, and ready to go to Church, where his heart always was. Mine ſhall erect a monument to him within myſelf, as laſting as my life. He had a regard for me—but, alas! for whom had he not? His cathedral, his dioceſe, all Italy, even Berlin, has experienced his liberalities. The King of Pruſſia honoured him with ſingular eſteem, and all the learned of Europe admired his zeal and his talents.

He had a conciliating turn of mind;—all the Proteſtants loved him, though he often told them ſevere truths. It is to be regretted that he did not leave ſome conſiderable work, inſtead of writing only detached pieces. He would have increaſed the Benedictine

nedictine Library, already so voluminous; and being one of the most distinguished members of the Order of St. Benedict, he would have enriched the Church with his productions.

If Poets are susceptible of friendships, Monf. Voltaire will regret him. They corresponded amicably—genius sought after genius. For me, who can only admire great men, and regret the loss of them, I shall shed tears upon the tomb of our illustrious Cardinal. *Quando inveniemus parem* * ?

I have the honour to be, &c.

Convent of the Holy Apostles,
13th January, 1755.

LETTER LXXXV.
TO A PAINTER.

WHILE there is expression in your pictures, my dear Sir, you may applaud yourself for your work. That is the essence of the art, and renders a number of faults excusable, which would not be forgiven in an ordinary Painter.

* When shall we find his equal?

I have

I have spoken of your talents to his Eminence Cardinal Porto-Carrero, and according to your desire, he will recommend you in Spain; but nothing will make you better known than your own genius;—one must be born a Painter, as well as a Poet. Carrache, notwithstanding the spirit of his pencil, would have produced no work worthy of attention, if he had not possessed that rapture which inspires with enthusiasm and ardour.

We see in his pictures a soul which speaks, which animates and inspirits: From the strength of admiration, we think we can become Carrache himself, and be filled with the justness of his images.

How the spirit of that great man, whom you have chosen for a model, breathes in you! You will revive him again upon the canvas! If you were only his shadow, you would deserve to be esteemed: the shadow of a great man has some reality.

Nature ought always to be the model for every man who paints; and to execute it well, no efforts are necessary. Painters, like Poets, produce Monsters, when

they

they ſtrain their genius in compoſing. When a man of genius is in a proper diſpoſition for executing a work, he feels himſelf hurried on by an irreſiſtible propenſity to ſeiſe the pen and the pencil, and give himſelf up to its inclination, without which he has neither expreſſion nor taſte.

Rome is undoubtedly the true ſchool to form a painter; but whatever trouble he takes, he will never riſe above mediocrity, unleſs he has genius.

It is time for me to have done; a counſellor of the Holy Office is not a painter, and we have every thing to loſe, when we ſpeak of what we know only imperfectly.

I am, Sir, &c.

LETTER LXXXVI.

TO MONSIGNOR AYMALDI.

YOU have reaſon to be ſurpriſed, my Lord, at the happy alliance which is henceforth to unite the houſes of Bourbon and Auſtria. There are prodigies in politicks

ticks as well as in nature: and Benedict XIV. on learning this furprifing news, had reafon for exclaiming, *O admirabile commercium**!

M. de Bernis has immortalifed himfelf by this political phenomenon, having had jufter views than Cardinal Richelieu.

By this means we fhall have no more wars in Europe, except when they grow tired of having peace; and the king of Pruffia, though always thirfting after glory, will not feek to make conquefts. But I fee Poland at his mercy; and becaufe a hero equally valiant and fortunate loves to aggrandife himfelf, he will one day take part of it, if that part be only the town of Dantzick. Poland itfelf may perhaps lend a helping hand to fuch a revolution, by not watching fufficiently at home, and fplitting into a thoufand different factions. The patriotick fpirit is no longer fufficient among the Polanders to animate them to defend their country at the expence of their lives. They are too often from home, to retain their national fpirit. It is only in England that the fpirit

---

* Admirable connection!

of patriotism is never extinguished, because it is founded on principle.

Europe has always had some warlike Monarch, jealous of extending his territories, or gathering laurels: sometimes a Gustavus, sometimes a Sobieski, sometimes a Louis the Great, sometimes a Frederick. Arms more than talents have aggrandised empires, because mankind have known that there is nothing of such energy as the law of the strongest, the *ultima ratio regum*.

Happily we feel none of these calamities here: all is in peace, and every one relishes its fruits deliciously; and as I eminently taste the pleasure of assuring you of all my esteem, and all my attachment.

LETTER LXXXVII.

TO THE ABBE NICOLINI.

SIR,

I WAS extremely sorry that I was not at the Convent of the Holy Apostles, when you came to favour me with a visit before your departure. Alas! I was upon the

the banks of the Tiber, which the ancient Romans magnified as they did their triumphs; for as to its length or breadth, it is but an ordinary river.

This is a walk which I have a particular liking to, from the ideas it infpires me with on the grandeur and declenfion of the Romans. I call to mind the times when thefe fierce defpots held the world in chains, and when Rome had as many Gods as they had vices and paffions.

I then fhrink back into my cell, where I employ myfelf about Chriftian Rome, and where, though the loweft in the houfe of God, I labour for its utility: but it is a work which is prefcribed, and therefore tedious; for in ftudying, a man commonly loves what he performs freely.

I dare not fpeak to you of the death of our common friend:—That would be to tear open a too-tender wound. I came too late to hear his laft words. He is regretted like one of thofe fingular men of whom his age was not worthy, and who poffeffed all the candour of the primitive times.

It

It is said that he has left some pieces of poetry worthy of the greatest masters. He never mentioned them, which is the more extraordinary, as Poets are seldom more discreet with regard to their writings, than to their merit in other respects.

For some time we have had a swarm of young Frenchmen here, and you may believe that I have seen them with much pleasure. My apartment was not large enough to hold them; they all did me the favour to come and see me, because they had been told that there was a Monk in the Convent of the Holy Apostles who had a particular regard for France, and every one that came from thence. They all spoke together, and it was an earthquake that gave me much pleasure.

They do not like Italy too much, because it is not yet quite Frenchified; but I comforted them, by assuring them that in time they would complete the metamorphosis, and that I was already more than half a Frenchman.

I have the honour to be, &c.
Rome, 24th July, 1756.

LETTER LXXXVIII.

TO MR. STUART, A SCOTCH GENTLEMAN.

IF you are not affected by the fluctuation of the waves which furround you, I will reproach you keenly for your inconftancy: inattention to an old friend, who has been always attached to you, is not to be forgiven. Your conduct reminds me of what I have often thought, that the principal nations of Europe refembled the elements.

The Italian, according to this fimilitude, reprefents the fire, which, always in action, flames and fparkles; the German may be compared to the earth, which, notwithftanding its denfity, produces good pulfe and excellent fruits; the French to the air, whofe fubtlety leaves not a trace behind; the Englifh to the fickle wave, which changes every inftant.

A fkilful Minifter, with addrefs, chains thefe elements as he finds neceffary, or makes them wreftle one againft the other, according to the interefts of his mafter. It is what we have feen more than once when

Europe was in combustion, and was agitated by reciprocal violences.

Human policy embroils or reconciles according to interest, having nothing more at heart than to govern or aggrandife. Christian policy, on the contrary, knows not the criminal art of sowing divisions; its greatest success is in preventing them. I can set no value upon policy which is not founded on equity, for that is Machiavelism put into action: but I have the most advantageous idea of a policy which is sometimes quiet, sometimes active; is governed by prudence; meditates, calculates, foresees, and, after having recalled the past, reflects upon the present, glances into futurity, and having all times in view, becomes active, or remains inactive.

It is absolutely necessary that a good Politician should be perfectly acquainted with history, and the age in which he lives; he should know the degree of strength and spirit possessed by those characters who appear on the stage of the world; to intimidate them if they are weak, to oppose them if they have courage, and to mislead them if they are rash.

A knowledge of men rather than of books, is the science of a good Politician; and it is of consequence in his affairs to know those perfectly whom he is to employ. Some are only proper for speaking, while others have courage which fits them for action; and all depends upon not mistaking their characters. Many Politicians fail from having misplaced their confidence. There is no recovering a secret when it has once escaped, and it is better to commit a fault by being too reserved, than by an imprudent confidence: *What we do not speak, cannot be written.*

The fear of being betrayed renders him pusillanimous, who has too lightly laid open his heart. There are circumstances where the Politician should appear to say every thing, though he says nothing; and be able to mislead with address, without betraying the truth; for it is never lawful to vary from it.

It is not weakness to yield when we cannot do otherwise; it is then wisdom. All depends on knowing the proper moment, and the characters of those you have to deal with;

with; to forefee certainly the effect which refiftance could have in fuch circumftances.

Vanity often proves very hurtful to a Politician. When, impelled by refentment, we defire to triumph over our enemy, and are eafily entangled in difficulties, from not forefeeing the confequences.

He who would lead men, ought to fubdue his paffions, and oppofe a cool head to thofe who have the greateft warmth; it is that which makes us commonly fay, *that the world is the inheritance of the phlegmatick.*

The way to difconcert the moft impetuous adverfary, is by great moderation.

We fhould have much lefs quarrelling and fewer wars, were we only to calculate what quarrelling and fighting muft coft. It is not fufficient to have men and money at our difpofal; we muft know how to employ them, and reflect that fortune is not always in the hands of the ftrongeft. For a long time we have had nothing but a temporifing policy at Rome, becaufe we are weak, and the courfe of events is the happieft refource to extricate thofe who cannot refift. But as this is now a fecret of which no one

one is ignorant, and as our flowneſs in determining is generally known, it is not amiſs, but even proper, for a Pope now and then to be determined; not in things that may be diſputed, but in things that are juſt; without which the Sovereign Pontiffs would be certain of being oppreſſed every time they are threatened.

Unfortunately, war is neceſſary for ſome nations to become opulent; there are others, again, to whom it proves certain ruin: from all which I conclude, that a Miniſter who knows how to profit ably of circumſtances is truely a treaſure; and when a ſovereign has the happineſs to find ſuch a man, he ſhould preſerve him, notwithſtanding cabals.

I have been ſtammering upon a ſubject which you underſtand much better than I do; but one word leads to another, and inſenſibly we ſpeak of what we do not know.

Thus it happens in letter-writing.—We do not foreſee all that we ſhall ſay. The ſoul, when it comes to recoil upon itſelf, is aſtoniſhed, and with reaſon, at its fertility.

It is a ſtriking picture of the production of a world from nothing; for our thoughts, which did not exiſt a little before, ſuddenly ſtart into being, and make us ſenſible that the Creation is really not impoſſible, as ſome modern Philoſopers pretend. I leave you with yourſelf; you are much better than with me. Adieu.

Rome, 22 Auguſt, 1756.

LETTER LXXXIX.

TO THE REV. FATHER ***, APPOINTED CONFESSOR TO THE DUKE OF ***.

WHAT a charge! What a burthen! my deareſt friend. Is it for your deſtruction, or for your ſalvation, that Providence has appointed you to this formidable employment? That idea ought to make you tremble.

You aſk me what you ſhould do to diſcharge it properly?—Be an Angel.

All things prove ſhelves and ſnares for the Confeſſor of a Sovereign, if he has not patience to wait God's good time, gentleneſs to compaſſionate imperfections, and ſteadineſs to reſtrain paſſions. You ought to be filled with a ſuperior meaſure of the gifts of the Holy Ghoſt, ſo as to diffuſe ſometimes hopes, ſometimes fears, and always inſtruction. You ſhould have a zeal capable of ſtanding the ſevereſt teſt, and a ſpirit of juſtice to balance the intereſts of the people, and a Sovereign of whom you have the guidance. You ſhould firſt endeavour to know, whether the Prince whom you direct is inſtructed in the duties of Religion, and his obligations towards his ſubjects; for, alas! it is too common for Princes to come out of the hands of thoſe who had the forming of them, without any knowledge but what is ſuperficial. Next you ſhould oblige your penitent to inſtruct himſelf, and to draw inſtruction from its true ſources, not loading the memory with many lectures, but ſtudying by principles what Religion and Politicks require from a Governour.

There are excellent works upon this ſubject, and you ought not to be ignorant of them. I know one that was compoſed for

Victor-

Victor-Amadeus, and which has no other fault but that of being too diffuse, and exacting too much.

When the duke is solidly instructed, for he should not sleep over frivolous ceremonies, recommend to him to seek truth continually, and to love it without reserve. Truth should be the Sovereign's compass. It will be the means of getting rid of all informers and Courtiers, who support themselves in Courts by flattery and falsehood, and who are by a thousand degrees the most dangerous of all scourges; destroying Princes both in this world and the next.

Insist, without intermission, on the necessity of showing due respect to Religion, not by inspiring a spirit of persecution, but by recommending an Evangelical courage, which spares the person, but stops the scandal. Repeat frequently, that the life of a Sovereign, like his Crown, is very insecure, if he suffers jesting about the worship due to God, and does not put a stop to irreligion.

Endeavour by your firmness, by your representations, by your prayers, and even by your tears, to make the Prince whom you guide

guide diftinguifh himfelf by the goodnefs of his morals, and caufe them to flourifh in his kingdom, as they conftitute the tranquillity of citizens, and the happinefs of families, which is the feed of population.

Reprefent to him frequently, that his fubjects are his children, and that he fhould be a parent to them day and night, to help and comfort them; that he fhould not impofe taxes upon them, but in proportion to their wealth and induftry, fo as neither to expofe them to indigence nor defpair; and that a ready adminiftration of juftice is his indifpenfible duty.

If you do not engage him to fee every thing with his own eyes, you will do your duty only by halves. The people are not made happy but by entering into particulars, which it is impoffible to know, without defcending to make the enquiry.

Though the Great defpife the people, and do not reflect, that in a State the People comprehends every individual except the Sovereign, yet to you, let that People be ever prefent, as a facred portion with which the Prince should be constantly engaged; —a portion which makes the support of the throne, and which should be watched like the apple of the eye.

Make him sensible, that the life of a Sovereign is a life of trouble, and that recreations are only permitted to him, as to the rest of mankind, for a relaxation; teach him to know, that he ought to break off his Christian studies, and even his prayers, if he is wanted for the support of the state.

Speak to him of the dreadful account which he must render to God of his administration, and not of the judgement which History pronounces against bad Princes after their deaths. That is not a proper motive to actuate a religious Prince; for History is only the voice of men, which perisheth with them: but the living God, the punisher of crimes, is the object which should regulate the conduct of a Sovereign. It is of little consequence to most people, whether they are well or ill spoken of after their death; but the sight of an eternal and inflexible Judge makes the most awful impression upon the human mind.

You

You will not prescribe those vague penances which consist in simple prayers, but apply a remedy fit to heal the wounds which will be exposed to you; and particularly endeavour to discover what is his prevailing fault; without which you may confess for a whole age without knowing your penitent. If you would stop the course of an evil, you must go to the fountain-head.

Take great care not to step beyond the bounds of your ministry, and not to meddle, I do not say with any intrigue, but, with any business of the Court. It is most unworthy to see a Monk, who ought to appear only as a representative of Jesus Christ, dishonour that august function by sordid interest, or detestable ambition.

All your desires, all your views, should have the safety of the Prince, who places his confidence in you, for their sole object. Astonish him by an incorruptible virtue, always equally supported. If a Confessor does not make himself respectable, and especially in a Court, where they only seek pretences for not being Christians, he authorises thorifes vices, and expofes himfelf to be defpifed.

Inculcate into the mind of the Prince, that he muft be anfwerable to God for all the employments he beftows, and all the evil which is done in confequence of his making an improper choice. Reprefent to him particularly, the danger of nominating ignorant or vicious people to ecclefiaftical dignities, and nourifhing their effeminacy and covetoufnefs by giving them a plurality of benefices. Perfuade him to feek out merit, and to recompenfe thofe who write for the good of the Public, and for Religion. Teach him to fupport his dignity, not by pride, but by a magnificence proportioned to the extent of his dominions, his forces, and his revenues; and to defcend, at the fame time, from his rank, to humanife himfelf with his people, and to fearch after true happinefs.

Place his duty frequently before his eyes, not with feverity nor with importunity, but with that charity, which, being the effufion of the Holy Spirit, never fpeaks but with prudence, feifes the proper feafon, and profits

fits by it. When a Prince is convinced of the knowledge and piety of his Confeffor, he hears him with good-nature, if his heart be not corrupted.

If your illuftrious pupil accufes himfelf of effential faults in adminiftration, fpeak to him in general terms, and you will come infenfibly to the point of making him confefs what you ought to know. You fhould often infift upon his hearing all his people, and doing them immediate juftice.

If you do not find yourfelf inclined to follow this plan, retire; for thefe are precepts which you cannot tranfgrefs, without rendering yourfelf guilty both in the fight of God and Man.

The function of an ordinary Confeffor does not attract the publick attention, but all eyes are fixed on the conduct of the man who is Confeffor to a Sovereign. When in the tribunal of penitence, you cannot be too exact, in not allowing any one to approach to the Sacraments, whofe fcandalous life muft render him unworthy in the eyes of the Publick. There are not two Gofpels, one for the Sovereign, and another for the people:

people: both will be equally judged by one unalterable law, becaufe the law of the Lord remaineth eternally.

Princes are not the images of God by their power and authority only, which they hold of him alone; they are fo likewife by the virtues which they fhould poffefs, in order to be proper reprefentatives of Him. A people fhould be able to fay of their Sovereign, " He governs like a Deity, with " wifdom, clemency, and equity;" for Sovereigns are accountable to their fubjects for their conduct; not that they ought to difclofe the fecrets of the Cabinet, but it is their duty to do nothing which can miflead the people.

Of all things, take care not to falfify the truth, either from weaknefs or any worldly motive. There is no capitulating with the law of God; it has the fame force at all times, and is actuated by one unvaried fpirit. The zeal of the great Ambrofius with regard to the Emperour Theodofius, is extolled by the Church as highly at prefent as it was formerly; for fhe neither changes in her morals nor opinions.

I pray

I pray to God, with all my heart, that he may support you, and enlighten you in so hazardous an employment, where you ought not to be an ordinary man, but a Heavenly guide. You will then live as a hermit, in the midst of the great world; as a truely religious man, in a dwelling where there is commonly but little Religion; as a Saint, in a place which would destroy the men of God, if the Lord was not every where with his Elect.

I embrace you, and am, &c.

Rome, 26th April, 1755.

LETTER XC.

TO THE PRELATE CERATI.

My Lord,

AT last the Chapter of Dominicans, at which our Holy Father solemnly presided, is over, and the Rev. Father Boxadors, equally distinguished by his birth and merit, hath been elected Superior General. He will govern with much wisdom and honesty, as an enlightened man who is acquainted with mankind, and knows

that

that they are not to be governed imperioufly.

Benedict XIV. who opened the Seffion with a difcourfe the moft eloquent and highly complimentary to the Order of St. Dominick, which has always been remarkable for the underftanding and virtue of its Members, defired to have the Rev. Father Richini for General, a truely modeft and learned Monk; but notwithftanding his prefence, and all his wifhes, he could not fucceed.

The Pope took it very well; and when going away faid with a fmile, " That the " Holy Therefa having afked our Saviour " wherefore a Carmelite, who he had re- " vealed to her fhould be chofen General, " had loft his election, he anfwered her, " *I was for him, but the Monks were againft* " *him.* It is not aftonifhing then, added " our Holy Father, that the will of his " Vicar hath not had its effect."

All the world knows that we too often refift the Holy Spirit, and that mankind daily defeat the intentions of the deity by their wicked ways.

Father Bremond is little regretted, although he was extremely affable and virtuous. His Order reproached him with having a blind condefcenfion for a brother who governed him, and whom I always diftrufted becaufe he appeared to me to be a flatterer. It is feldom that men of that character are not falfe. Your fweetened language is rarely the language of fincerity.

I pitied poor Bremond, without daring to blame him. What man in employment but has been deceived?

Many people judge unkindly of the Great, and efpecially when they are not great themfelves. The circumftance of men in high ftations being befet with cares and embaraffments is not attended to; though that fhould in fome meafure excufe them, as they cannot fee all with their own eyes. Happy he who only views Greatnefs at a diftance, like a mountain which he has no inclination to climb!

I have the honour to be, &c.

Rome, 29 July, 1756.

LETTER XCI.

TO AN ENGLISH LORD.

MY Lord, inftructed as you are in the imperfections of human Nature, the variety of opinions, the caprice of tafte, and the force of cuftoms, I cannot conceive why you fhould be aftonifhed at the form of our Government. I do not pretend to juftify it, as it neither favours commerce, agriculture, nor population; that is to fay, what forms the effence of publick felicity: but do you think there are no inconveniencies in other countries?

It is true, we are under a torpid Government, which excites neither emulation nor induftry; but I fee you Englifhmen under the yoke of a populace, who drag you as they pleafe, and who by their impetuofity, which cannot be reftrained, become your Sovereigns: I fee other nations, fuch as the Polanders, plunged in anarchy, and the Ruffians under defpotifm: not to mention the Turks, who dare not fpeak for fear of their all-abfolute Sultan.

It is generally imagined, though I do not know why, that the Ecclesiastical Government is a sceptre of iron; yet whoever has read its history, cannot be ignorant that the Christian Religion has abolished slavery; that in those countries where it still unhappily prevails, as in Poland and Hungary, the Peasants, who are under the government of Bishops, are not bondsmen; and that, in a word, nothing is more gentle than the dominion of the Popes. Besides their never engaging in war, being necessarily Princes of Peace, they trouble nobody either for taxes, or their way of thinking.

There are certain Inquisitions which have caused the Priests to be branded with the name of Persecutors. But, besides that the Monarchs who authorized them, were equally guilty with the instigators, Rome was never seen to indulge in the barbarous pleasure of burning their citizens for want of Faith, or because some improper discourse had escaped them. Jesus Christ, expiring upon the Cross, far from exterminating those who blasphemed him, sollicited their pardon with his Father: *Pater ignosce illis**.

One

* Father, forgive them.

One thing is certain, that although some Ministers of God have sometimes declared for blood and carnage, they have only done it by an enormous abuse of Religion, which, having charity for its essence, preaches up meekness and peace.

Yet, wheresoever I look round the world, I see that, in the midst of our indigence and apathy, we are still the people who live most happily. This is owing, it is true, to the goodness of the soil and climate, which furnishes us abundantly with the necessaries of life.

If our Government had more activity, there would certainly be more vigour and circulation in the Ecclesiastical State: But who hath told us that the Government would not then become despotick? The luke-warmness of the Popes, who are commonly too old to undertake or execute, makes at once our misfortune and our happiness. They leave the country to produce what it pleases, without attending either to its culture or improvement; but they crush nobody under the weigh of taxes, and every one

one is sure of remaining in peace at home, without the least molestation.

Rich countries are taxed in proportion to their wealth; and I know not, in fact, whether it is better to inhabit a country flourishing by its industry, and obliged to pay exorbitant burthens, which leave only the means of subsisting; or to live in a place without this circulation, but in happy ease. It appears to me that every individual, separately, chooses rather to gain little with nothing to pay, than to gain much, and pay almost the whole. I prefer having only twenty-five sequins of my own, to the happiness of possessing a hundred out of which I must pay ninety.

We are frequently misled by specious advantages in what we say upon Government. The whole world undoubtedly requires that we should labour and be active, lending our hands to one another from the most distant parts of the globe, and by keeping up correspondences that we should support a just equilibrium, or at least a happy harmony: Yet that does not hinder but there may be a little corner in the world which may

may be happy, without taking a part in all these enterprises and revolutions, and we are in that little intrenchment where the serpents of Discord do not hiss, and where Tyranny doth not exercise her cruelties.

The human mind is always in motion, because man is perpetually agitated: Men never love to see countries rest in torpid indolence. Thus conquerours, who ravage kingdoms, who plunder, who kill, and usurp, please them much more than those beings who, remaining fixed in one place, lead an uniform life, and do not, by their revolutions, present them with any interesting spectacle on the theatre of the world.

Yet the life celebrated by Philosophers and Poets is not a life of tumult; in order to render men happy, they banish avarice and ambition from their minds; and in this they agree with the true Christians, who preach up disinterestedness and humanity.

I assure you, I have often estimated every kind of Government, and I should be puzzled to decide which is the best. None of them are without their inconveniences;
and

and at this we should be the less surprised, since the universe itself, though governed by infinite wisdom, is subject to the strangest revolutions. Sometimes we are crushed by thunder, sometimes afflicted by calamities, and almost always vexed either by shocks of the elements, or by the plague of insects: in the heavenly country only all will be perfect, and there we shall find neither evils nor dangers.

A little less enthusiasm for your country, Sir, would make you allow that there are abuses in it as in others But how expect an Englishman not to be an enthusiast in favour of his country? You will tell me, that the liberty and property of your citizens are singularly respected with you; and I will answer, that these two prerogatives, which essentially constitute happiness, and which ought never to be invaded, remain equally inviolate in the dominions of the Pope. There every one is allowed to enjoy his property in peace, to go and come as he pleaseth, without being molested. The rigours of authority are unknown in the Ecclesiastical States, and you may say,

that

that the Superiors rather entreat than command. Do not imagine, from thefe obfervations, that I am an apologift for a Government fo defective as our's: I know its defects as well as you; but think that there is not an adminiftration in the univerfe of which we may not fpeak both good and ill. May the republican love republicks, and the fubjects of monarchs love monarchies, and then all will be as it ought! As for me, I act as I ought, when I affure you of the refpect, &c.

Rome, 27th September, 1756.

LETTER XCII.

TO A PHYSICIAN.

I Am grieved, my dear Friend, that your domeftick affairs are ftill in fo bad a fituation, and that your wife, by her exceffive expences, labours continually to make them worfe. There is nothing but patience and mildnefs which can affect her. Gain her confidence, and you will afterwards gain what you pleafe. You fhould never moleft a wife, whatever faults she may have committed, but find some means capable of opening her eyes. Speak reason to her; seem to enter into her views so as not to have the appearance of contradicting her; and insensibly, by candid representations, by good treatment, by sensible reasonings, by the effusions of the heart, she may be brought to relish the morals you preach to her; but you must not assume either a pedantick manner, or the tone of a moraliser.

Above all things, do not complain of your wife before your children, but still less before your servants. They will acquire the habit of no longer respecting her; perhaps they may despise her.

Women deserve attention; and the more so, as their peevishness is almost always owing to the temper of husbands, or domestick vexations. Their tender forms require attention, as well as their situation, which does not permit them to divert their cares so easily as we can do, whose lives are divided between business and study. While the husband goes abroad on business or pleasure, the wife remains confined at home,
necessarily

necessarily employed in minute attentions which are consequently teazing. Women who love reading have a resource, but they cannot be always reading: besides, almost every woman who reads much is infected with vanity.

I advise you to recommend to her creditors, to come frequently to persecute her, when she is in their debt. She will soon grow tired of their visits, and then you should take occasion to show her, that there cannot be a greater misfortune than to be in debt when we cannot pay. You will engage her attention by mentioning the necessity of saving something for her children. She loves them tenderly, and that motive will be the best lesson which can be given her.

I formerly knew an old officer at Pesaro, who had suffered much by the passionate freaks of his wife. When she fell into a rage, he remained immoveable, and did not speak one word; and this silence very soon cooled her passion. The passionate are to be disarmed by mildness.

How pleased am I, my dear Doctor, that I am married to my cell! It is a quiet companion,

panion, which does not fpeak one word, which does not put my patience to the trial, and which I find always the fame at whatever hour I return; always tranquil and ready to receive me. The vexations of the Monks are nothing, when compared with thofe of people who live in the world; but it is neceffary that every one fhould fuffer patiently, and reflect that this life is not eternal. St. Jerome faid, that he advifed marriage to thofe only who were fearful in the night, that they might have a companion to keep up their courage; but as he was never fearful, he never inclined to marry.

I am glad that your eldeft fon has fuch uncommon fagacity. As the temper of the youngeft is more referved, you muft try it in order to make him fhow himfelf. The talent of a father is to multiply himfelf, and to appear to his children under different forms: To one, as a mafter—to another, as a friend.

The confidence which the firft people of the town place in you does them honour. They muft have known, from frequent cures

cures, that the reproaches against physicians are not always well founded. The fashion is to be merry at their expence; but for my part, I am convinced that there is more understanding among them than almost all the other professions; and that their science is not so conjectural as is commonly thought: but man, ingenious in deluding himself, says, that it is never Death, but always the Physician that kills. Besides, what learned man never deceives himself? We should not see so many sophisms and paradoxes in books were it not that writers are fallible, though they know a great deal.

What I say to you, my dear Doctor, is the more generous on my part, because I enjoy the most perfect health, and have no need of any physician. I take my chocolate every morning, lead a frugal life, use a great deal of snuff, and walk frequently; and with such a regimen, one may live an age; but I am not desirous of long life.

Love me always as your best friend, the friend of your family, and as one who most sincerely wishes to see you happy.

My compliments to your dear wife,
whom

whom I wish to see as reasonable in her expences as you are:—that time will come. The happiness of this life consists in always hoping.

Rome, 30 September, 1756.

LETTER XCIII.

TO THE SAME.

YOU will see, my Friend, by the enclosed memorial of your colleagues, who tear each other to pieces, that study does not exempt us from the weaknesses incident to human nature.

Yet, the learned ought to set an example of moderation, and leave quarrels and jealousies to the vulgar, as their proper element. Every Age has produced literary combats very humiliating to sense and reason. The merit of one is not the same in another, and I cannot see why envy should be so exasperated as to decry those who have reputation. I would rather never have read in my life, than conceive the least

least hatred against a writer. If he writes well, I admire him; if badly, I excuse him, because I imagine he did his best.

The greater the number of mean souls who rank themselves in the list of writers, the more they detest and tear one another in pieces. Men of genius, like the generous mastiff, despise the insults of little curs. The truely great never reply to criticks;—satire is best answered by silent contempt.

Men of superficial knowledge are much more exposed to these squabbles than the truely learned, because their application is quite different. The learned are too much absorbed in study to hearken to the whispers of jealousy; while the others, like light troops, are scattered about upon the watch.

The French have a great deal of these hateful disputes in their writings, from their having many more superficial than profound authors. Their agreeable vivacity leads them to trivial pursuits, rather than to the study of the Sciences: from a dread that

that their gaiety muſt be laid under reſtraint, and their liberty be loſt in intenſe
application. The learned man writes for
poſterity, and the ſuperficial for the preſent
age; he is in a hurry to gain reputation
for the immediate gratification of ſelf-love,
preferring the applauſe of a day to a more
laſting glory.

I am delighted to hear that your remon-
ſtrances have at laſt made an impreſſion upon your wife: ſhe will poſſibly at laſt become a miſer. But take care of that, for
ſhe will perhaps make you die of hunger;
and a Phyſician preſcribes only ſtrict regimen
to his patients.

I have ſcarce time to read the work you
mentioned; but as you ſpeak ſo highly of its
latinity, I will endeavour to glance it over.
There are ſome books which I run over in
the twinkling of an eye, others which I dive
into ſo as to loſe nothing; but it depends
upon the ſubjects, and the manner of treat-
ing them.

I love a work whoſe chapters, like ſo
many avenues, lead agreeably to ſome
intereſt-

interesting prospect. When I see the road crooked, and the ground rugged, I reject it at the beginning; and go no farther, unless the importance of the subject makes me forget the manner in which it is delivered.

I leave you to visit an English Lord, who thinks, as he speaks, with energy. He cannot conceive how Rome can canonize men who have lived holy lives; as if we did not judge of men by their lives, and as if God had not promised the Kingdom of Heaven to those who faithfully accomplish the Law.

I believe, however, that that excellent work of the Holy Father, *On the Canonization of Saints*, will open his eyes; he esteems the Pontiff greatly, and has an high opinion of his writings. Adieu!

CONVENT of the HOLY APOSTLES,
5th November, 1756.

LETTER XCIV.

TO THE ABBE LAMI.

I WISH, my dear Abbé, for the honour of your country and of Italy, that the History of Tuscany, which is going to be published, may correspond with its title.

What excellent matter to handle, if the writer, equally judicious and delicate, shows the arts springing from this country, where they had been buried during so many ages; and if he paints in proper colours the Medicis, to whom we owe this inestimable advantage!

History brings together all ages and all Mankind into one point of view, presenting a charming landscape to the mental eye. It gives colour to the thoughts, soul to the actions, and life to the dead; and brings them again upon the stage of the world, as if they were still living; but with this difference, that it is not to flatter, but to judge them.

Formerly History was but badly written, and even at this day our Italian Authors are not much improved. They only compile events and dates, without characterizing the genius either of nations or heroes.

The generality of men look upon History with a cursory glance, as they would on a piece of Flanders tapestry. They are content to see characters shining by the vivacity of the colouring, without thinking of the head which drew the design, or the hand which executed it. And thus they think they see every thing, while they see nothing.

It is impossible to profit by history, if we are attentive only to Princes, battles, and exploits, passing in review before us; but I do not know more instructive reading, if we consider the progress of events, and observe how they were conducted; when we analyse the talants and designs of those people who set all in motion, and transport ourselves to the ages and countries in which such memorable actions happened.

History

Hiftory affords an inexhauftible fund for reflections. Every action fhould be weighed, not with a minute examination, which doubts of every thing, but with a critical eye which will not be deceived. It is feldom that young people profit by the reading of Hiftory, becaufe it is given to them as a kind of exercife calculated folely for the memory; inftead of being told, that it is the foul, and not the eyes, which ought to be employed in fuch a ftudy.

Then they will obferve fome men highly praifed, who were the difgrace of human nature; others who were perfecuted, yet were the glory of their country, and the age in which they lived. Then they will know the fprings of emulation, and the dangers of ambition; they will fee felf-intereft the *primum mobile* in cities, courts, and families.

Hiftorians rarely make reflections, that they may leave their readers at leifure to analyfe and judge of the people of whom they fpeak.

In all the hiftories of the world, we find people who fcarcely appear on the fcene, yet

yet behind the curtain set all in motion. These escape not the attentive reader, who gives them the honour of what flattery has too often ascribed to the man in office. Almost all Princes and Ministers have some secret Agent by whom they are moved, and who is only to be discovered by analysing them.

We may likewise say, that some of the greatest events which have astonished the world, have frequently taken rise from persons obscure, both in rank and extraction. Many women who appeared only as the wives of Princes or Ambassadors, and who are not even mentioned in History, have frequently been the cause of some of the noblest exploits. Their counsels have prevailed and been followed; and the husbands have had all the honour of enterprises which was due to the sagacity of their wives.

Tuscany furnishes much excellent matter, which an able Historian might display in a most lively and striking manner. That period where we see Princes of such contracted power as the family of Medici, reviving

viving the arts, and spreading them all over Europe, will not be the least interesting. When I reflect upon this æra, it seems like a new world rising out of a chaos; a new Sun coming to give light to the different nations. O that this work, my dear Abbé, had fallen into your hands! You would have given it all the spirit it was capable of. Adieu! Somebody is coming to besiege me, and I won't be blocked up—they are visits of politeness, which should be respected.

ROME, 8th November, 1756.

LETTER XCV.

TO COUNT ***.

I Cannot sufficiently express my joy, my dear Count, when I think you are going on steadily in the paths of virtue, and that you are sufficiently master of yourself, to keep your senses, passions, and heart in order.

Yes, we will make that little excursion we projected. Your company is become my delight, since you have become a new man.

I will

I will prefent you to the Holy Father with pleafure, when you come to Rome; and I will proteft to you he will be happy to fee you, efpecially when he knows that you apply yourfelf to proper ftudies. You will find him as lively as if he was only five and-twenty.

Gaiety is the balm of life; and what induces me to believe that your piety will be lafting, is, your being always of a chearful temper. They become infenfibly tired of virtue, who become tired of themfelves. Every thing then becomes a burthen, and the whole concludes with finking into a difmal mifanthropy, or the greateft diffipation. I approve much of your bodily exercifes: they enliven the fpirits, and make us fit for every thing: I take as much exercife as the gloomy profeffion of a Monk allows.

When you come to vifit me, I will tell you all that the implacable Marchionefs alledges in her own vindication for not feeing you. I always thought that her particular devotion would not allow her to do fo good an action: fhe would fupport her conduct by by vanity. You cannot imagine how difficult it is for some devotees to acknowledge themselves in the wrong.

As for you, stop where you are. You have written to her; you have spoken to her; and certainly that is enough; especially as St. Paul tells us, that we should be at peace with all the world, if possible—*si fieri potest*. He knew that there are some unsociable people, with whom it is impossible to live cordially.

I embrace you with all my heart, &c.

LETTER XCVI.

TO R. P. LUCIARDI, A BARNABITE.

MOST REV. FATHER,

YOUR decision is perfectly conformable to the Councils, and I should have been much astonished if it had been otherwise, considering the long time that I have been acquainted with your extensive knowledge and your judicious opinions.

Besides the excellent books which you always have in your library, you constantly have

have with you the reverend P. Gerdil, whose learning and modesty deserve the greatest praise.

Take care of your health, for the sake of Religion and our own interests.

The city of Turin where you live, certainly knows the value of possessing you, for it is a place where merit is esteemed and cherished.

I make a scruple of detaining you longer from your studies and exercises of piety, and therefore conclude without ceremony, by assuring you most cordially that

I am, &c.

Rome, 3d December, 1756.

LETTER XCVII.
TO A DIRECTOR OF NUNS.

I Do not congratulate you upon your employment, but I will endeavour that you shall acquit yourself with all possible prudence and charity.

Take my advice, and go very seldom into the Parlour: it is a place of idle conversation, senseless tales, and little slanders,
and

and your frequenting it cannot fail to excite jealoufies; for if you fee one oftener than another, they will come fecretly to hear you from a fpirit of curiofity, which muft produce cabals and parties, and the leaft word you fpeak will have a thoufand commentaries.

Secondly, you cannot remove the idle fcruples you will often hear of, except by defpifing them, and never liftening to them more than twice.

Thirdly, accuftom the Nuns never to fpeak of any thing which does not regard themfelves, while at confeffion, becaufe they will otherwife make the confeffion of their neighbours; and in confeffing one only, you will learn infenfibly the faults of the whole community.

Fourthly, endeavour conftantly to maintain peace in all their hearts, repeating inceffantly that Jefus Chrift is to be found only in the bofom of peace.

Frequently reflect, that if there is luft in the eyes of all men, as St. John tells us, there is a luft in the tongues and ears of many Nuns. Have you fkill to cure them?

If

If it is not proper to prescribe absolute silence, it is at least necessary to prohibit malicious discourse, where they amuse themselves at the expence of their neighbours.

Respect the tenderness of the sex, which requires condescension in governing them; and show some indulgence to the poor recluse labouring in spirit, so as not to add to the yoke, already sufficiently heavy from the burthen of an eternal solitude.

Our Holy Father has known their wants, by allowing them to visit each other once a year. Whatever is done from a principle of charity deserves to be praised.

There are occasions where it will be necessary to exercise all your firmness, and without which you will not be Director, but directed. Some Devotees have the address to lead him who hath the care of their conscience; they do this with an air of perfect piety, without seeming to intend it.

If you neglect these hints, you will repent; but you will do better if you appear only at Confession, or in the Pulpit, and at the Altar. You will be much more respected.

ed. There are few Directors who do not lose a great deal by making themselves too much known. It is great wisdom never to appear among them unseasonably. Ask me nothing further upon this article, for I have told you all that I know. Adieu!

Convent of the Holy Apostles,
19th December, 1756.

LETTER XCVIII.

TO THE COUNT GENORI.

MY books, my monastick exercises, my employment, all join to oppose the pleasure I should otherwise have in visiting you. Besides, what would you do with a Monk whose time is continually interrupted with reading and prayer, which would break in upon our walks and our conversations?

I am so accustomed to my hours of solitude and application, that I believe I could not exist without them.

All the happiness of a Monk consists in being alone, in praying and in studying. I have no other; and I prefer it to all the
pleasures

pleasures of the world. The conversation of the learned or some of my friends is infinitely precious to me, provided they do not break in upon my time. I never proposed to be the slave of the minute in the hours which I can dispose of, because I hate every thing which is trifling; but I love order, and I see nothing else which can preserve the harmony of the soul and the senses.

Where there is no order, there can be no peace. Tranquillity is the daughter of Regularity, and it is by regularity that man can shut himself up within the sphere of his duty. All the inanimate creation preach up regularity; the stars perform their course periodically, and the plants revive at the moment which is marked out to them. We can tell the instant the day should appear, and it doth not fail; we know the moment of the night, and then darkness covers the earth.

The true Philosopher never perverts the order of time, unless obliged by occupations or customs which require it.

To return, Sir, to Natural History, which you mentioned to me: it is certain we have

have studied it less than Antiquity, although the former is much more useful than the latter. Nevertheless, Italy at every step presents wherewithal to exercise and satisfy the curiosity of Naturalists. Phenomena may be seen in Italy, that are not to be seen elsewhere; and people who are said to be less superstitious than the Italians, would instantly take them to be miracles.

A French Abbé, who has been here for some time, and whom I got acquainted with by means of Cardinal Paffionei, was in the greatest astonishment at seeing the wonders which Nature every where presented to him. I shall always remember a walk which I had with him near the Villa Mattei, and which lasted five hours, though no great distance, because he stopped every instant. He has knowledge, and such a taste for Natural History, that he is attracted by an insect or a flint, without being able to tear himself from them. I was afraid he would petrify himself with looking so much upon stones; and I must say I should have been a greater loser, for his conversation is exceedingly engaging and chearful. This is

the

the Abbé who has written againſt the ſyſtems of Monſ. Buffon. How much longer would he not have remained, if he had had the happineſs of being with you?

I have the honour to be, with the moſt lively gratitude, and moſt reſpectable attachment,

Your moſt humble, &c.

LETTER XCIX.

TO COUNSELLOR C***.

O Such compliments! If you knew how I love them, you would not make them.

What has been ſaid with regard to the perſon in queſtion, is only founded on envy and malice. Is there a man in office, or a man who hath written, that has not enemies? Libels and ſatires make an impreſſion only upon weak and badly-organiſed heads; and you will obſerve, that the moſt vicious and ſpotted characters are always

always moſt ready to believe calumny, and ſhow the greateſt reluctance to ſee thoſe whom they have offended.

Prejudice, however, is ſo common, that, according to the obſervation of the Holy Father, a thouſand recommendations are wanted to determine a man in office in favour of any perſon; but there needs one word only to make him change, or to provoke him. This is the ſtrongeſt proof of the depravity of the human heart.

We ſhould be obliged to ſee nobody, were we to ſhut our doors againſt all who have been ill ſpoken of. We ought to be very careful to avoid judging raſhly. It is ſhameful to paſs ſentence againſt our brother, when we have not ſufficient proofs to accuſe him.

Prejudice ruins a number of the Great, and eſpecially Devotees, who think they ought piouſly to give credit to all the evil which is ſpoken of their neighbour. They pretend to be ignorant that God hath expreſsly commanded us not to judge, leſt we be judged; and that it is leſs criminal in his eyes, to commit faults which we repent

repent of, than to accuse our brethren rashly.

The first rule of Christian charity is to believe no ill, if we have not seen it; and to be silent, if we have seen it.

Besides, if he whom they would prevent you from seeing, seeks the society of good people, it is a proof that he is not such a libertine as they pretend, or that he is inclined to reform. Perhaps his salvation depends upon the good example you will set him; therefore I would not have you reject him.

Charity does not judge like the world; because the world almost never fails to judge amiss.

I am, &c.

Convent of the Holy Apostles.

E T.

LETTER C.

TO THE ABBE L***.

SIR,

SINCE you confult me upon the Difcourfe which I lately heard, I muft tell you with my ufual freedom, that I found fome excellent things in it, but did not like that affectation by which it was enervated. It looks like a work which had been made and painted at a Lady's toilette. For the future, let your heart fpeak when you mount the Pulpit, and you will fpeak well. Fancy fhould be employed only to make a border for the painting, but you have made it the foundation of your Difcourfe.

A good Orator fhould keep a medium between the Italian and French; that is to fay, between a Giant and a Dwarf.

Do not let yourfelf be fpoiled by the manners of the Age, or you will never be able to get rid of that affected eloquence which tortures both words and thoughts. It is of importance to a young man of abilities to receive fuch advice, and above all

all to follow it; and I depend upon your modesty for taking it in good part. I am, with all possible desire of seeing you a perfect Orator,

Sir, your's, &c.

ROME, 10th of the Month.

LETTER CI.

TO PRINCE SAN-SEVERO.

I AM always in admiration at your new discoveries. By what you have created, you have produced a second world from the first. This will distract our Antiquaries, who persuade themselves that there is nothing excellent or engaging which is not very old.

It is undoubtedly very proper that we should value antiquity; but I think we should not make ourselves such slaves to it, as to exalt beyond measure a thing which is despicable in itself, only because it was dug out of Adrian's garden.

The Ancients had things for common use as well as we; and if they are to be valued

valued merely becaufe of their antiquity, the earth in this quality deferves our firft homage, for furely its antiquity is not to be queftioned.

I neither love enthufiafm nor infenfibility: thofe only who keep the middle between thefe two extremes, can either fee or judge rightly. The cold indifference of the infenfible takes away all tafte and curiofity; and we ought to be poffeffed of either the one or the other, to examine and entitle us to pronounce.

Fancy, when not regulated, is much more dangerous than indifference. It dazzles the eye, and clouds the underftanding. Even Philofophy, of whom this fportive Deity fhould have no hold, daily feels the too fatal impreffion. Sophiftry, paradoxes, captious reafonings, compofe the train of our modern Philofophers, and have no other origin than Fancy. She takes wing as whim happens to lead, without having the leaft refpect either for truth or experience.

Your Excellency certainly knows this kind of writing, as you have frequent opportunities of reading the productions of the Times. England, which on account of its phlegm we should imagine had less fancy than other nations, has often published the most extravagant ideas. Its Philosophers have been still more distracted than our's, because they must have made greater efforts to surmount their natural character of reserve and taciturnity. Their imagination is like the coal which flames, and whose vapour disturbs the brain.

It is said, with reason, that the imagination is the mother of dreams, and even produces more than the night; but these are the more dangerous, as in giving way to them, we do not think we dream, while the morning is sure to undeceive us as to the illusions of the night.

I am always afraid of your chemical experiments hurting your health, for sometimes very terrible accidents happen from them. But when new experiments in Physics are to be made, a man runs into them without any dread of the consequences, like an Officer hurried

hurried on by his valour, who throws himself at all hazards into the midst of the fire.

I have the honour to be,
With respect and attachment, &c.

Rome, 13th January, 1757.

LETTER CII.

TO A PRELATE.

My Lord,

UNITE yourself with me, that we may revenge the memory of Sixtus Quintus. I was moved to a degree of warmth yesterday in supporting him against some who called him a cruel Pope, a Pontiff unworthy of reigning. It is astonishing how this character which has been bestowed upon him is supported, and what footing it has obtained in the world.

Is it reasonable to judge so great a man, without once reflecting on the times in which he lived, when Italy swarmed with robbers; when Rome was less secure than a forest, a foreſt, and modeſt women were inſulted in her ſtreets at mid-day?

The Severity of Sixtus Quintus, who is improperly called *Cruel,* would in ſuch circumſtances be at leaſt as pleaſing in the ſight of God, as the piety of Pius V.

We have ſeen that thouſands of men have been aſſaſſinated under the reign of ſome Popes, without the murtherers being brought to puniſhment: then was the time when it might have been ſaid with propriety, that the Popes were cruel: but when Sixtus Quintus put to death only about fifty robbers, to ſave the lives of his ſubjects, to re-eſtabliſh morals in the midſt of the cities, and ſecurity in the heart of the country, at a time when there was neither law, nor order, nor reſtraint; this was an act of juſtice and zeal, uſeful to the Public, and therefore agreeable to God.

I confeſs to you, that I am grieved when I ſee great men's characters become the fable of ignorant and prejudiced writers. Even poſterity, which is ſaid to be an impartial judge, has more than once been miſled by the reflections of an artful Hiſtorian, who

who seats himself upon the bench without authority, and pronounces according to his prejudices.

It is in vain to cry out calumny—the impreffion has been made—the book has been read, and the multitude judge only from the firft account. Thus *Gregorio Leti* has rendered the character of Sixtus Quintus hateful all over the world, inftead of reprefenting him as a Sovereign who was obliged to intimidate his people, and reftrain them by the moft ftriking examples of feverity.

Nothing is fo dreadful for a country as too mild a government. Crimes make a thoufand times more victims than well-timed punifhments. The Old Teftament is full of examples of juftice and terrour; and they were commanded by God himfelf, who furely cannot be accufed of cruelty.

I will certainly wait upon you the firft moment in my power; you may depend upon it, as upon the affection with which I fhall be all my life, &c.

CONVENT of the HOLY APOSTLES,
 8th April, 1757.

LETTER CIII.

TO A YOUNG MONK.

My Dear Friend,

THE advice you afk about your manner of ftudying, ought to be fuited to your difpofition and talents. If vivacity is your prevailing temper, it may be moderated by reading works of little imagination; but, on the contrary, if you find your thoughts languid, you fhould enliven yourfelf by reading books written with fpirit.

Do not burthen your memory with dates and facts, before you have arranged your ideas, and acquired a juftnefs in reafoning. You fhould accuftom yourfelf to think methodically, and to difpel, as much as poffible, the chimeras that may ftart up in your brain.

He who thinks only vaguely, is fit for nothing, becaufe nothing can be found capable of fixing him.

The foundation of your ftudies ought to be the knowledge of God and yourfelf.

By

By philosophising upon your nature, you will acknowledge an Existence, to whom you owe your creation; and by reflecting on the strayings of the imagination, and the wanderings of the heart, you will become sensible of the necessity of a Revelation, which hath revived the law of nature in a more lively and effectual manner.

- Then will you give yourself up without reserve to that science, which from reason and authority introduces us into the sanctuary of Religion; and there you will attain a knowledge of that heavenly doctrine revealed in the Scriptures, and interpreted by the Councils and Fathers of the Church.

Reading then will render true eloquence familiar to you, and you should take them early for models, so as to succeed afterwards in your manner of writing or preaching.

You will take the opportunity, when there are intervals in your exercises, to cast your eye on the finest fragments of the Orators and Poets, as St. Jerome did; that is to say, not as a man who made them his study, but as one who extracted from them the best passages, in order to improve his style, and to make them useful in the cause of Religion.

The Historians will next lead you by the hand from age to age, and show you the events and revolutions which have never ceased to employ and agitate the world: this will give you a constant opportunity of acknowledging and adoring a Providence which directs all according to its designs.

You will see in almost every page of History, how Empires and Emperors have been instruments of justice or mercy in the hands of God; how he exalted, and how he depressed them; how he created, and how he destroyed them, being Himself always unchangeably the same.

You should read over again in the morning what you read at night, so as to fix it in your memory; and in order to prevent your becoming a pedant, after a work of lively imagination, never fail to take up some more solid and phlegmatick composition.

This

This will compose your thoughts, which the productions of an elevated mind are apt to ferment, and will restrain the genius, which otherwise might be too easily hurried out of its proper sphere.

Endeavour to procure the conversation of learned men as much as you possibly can. Happily Providence has supplied you; for in almost all our Houses there are Monks who have studied to advantage.

Do not neglect the society of old men: their memories are furnished with many facts which they witnessed, and which make them repositories well worth examining. They resemble old books, that contain excellent matter, though badly bound, dusty, and worm-eaten.

Be not too fond of any work, authour, or sentiment, for fear of becoming a party-man; but when you prefer another, let it be because you find him one writer to more solid and truely excellent.

You ought to guard with great caution against prepossession and prejudice; but unfortunately, the more we ftudy, the more we are liable to be infected by them.

We become interefted in an Author who has written well, and infenfibly we praife and admire all his opinions, though they are perhaps very often fantaftical. Guard againft this misfortune, and be always more the friend of Truth, than of Plato or Scotus.

Refpect the fentiments of your Order, that you may not difturb the eftablifhed doctrines; yet I do not mean that you fhould be a flave to them. You ought not to be immoveable in any opinion but what relates to the Faith, and has been rendered facred by the concurrence of the whole Church. I have feen Profeffors who would rather fuffer death, than abandon the principles they imbibed in the Schools: my conduct with regard to them has been, always to pity and avoid them. Do not apply to fcholaftic erudition further than is neceffary to know the jargon of the Schools, and to confute the Sophifts; for, fo far
from

from being the essence of Theology, it is only the bark.

Avoid disputes, since nothing is cleared up by wranglings: but when opportunities offer, support truth and combat error with the arms which Jesus Christ and the Apostles have put into your hands, and which consist of mildness, persuasion, and charity. The mind is not to be taken by force, but to be gained by insinuation.

Do not fatigue your mental faculties, by giving up to immoderate study. Sufficient for the day is the labour thereof; and unless in a case of necessity, it is needless to anticipate the studies of the next, by prolonging your application in the night.

The man who regulates his time, and uniformly devotes only a few hours to study, advances much more than he who heaps up moment upon moment, and does not know when to stop. They who are of this character, commonly end by becoming only the title-pages of books, or a library turned upside down.

Without being attentive to minute trifles, love

love order; so that you may leave off till another time, when you no longer find yourself inclined to study. The Scholar should not labour like the ox that is yoked to the plough, nor like the mercenary who is paid by the day.

It is a bad custom to struggle continually against rest and sleep: that which is done against the grain, is never well done; and too earnest an application to any thing injures the health.

There are days and hours when we have no disposition for application; and then it is a folly to attempt it, unless in a case of necessity.

There is scarcely any book which does not favour of painful composition in some part of it, because the Author has often written when he should have rested.

The great art in studying is to know when it is proper to begin, and when to leave off; without which the head becomes heated, the spirits are either absorbed or exalted, so that we produce nothing but what is either languid or flighty. Learn to make a proper choice of books, that you
may

may know only what is excellent, and to make a good ufe of it. Life is too fhort to wafte in fuperfluous ftudies; and if we do not make hafte to learn, we fhall find ourfelves old without knowing any thing.

Above all things, pray to God to enlighten your mind; for there is no knowledge without his affiftance; and we are in utter darknefs, if we do not follow the Light which he hath revealed to us.

Dread becoming learned folely to gain a reputation; for befides that knowledge puffeth up, and charity edifieth, a Community becomes difgufted with thofe who make a parade of their learning.

Let events have their courfe, and let your merit procure your advancement. If employments do not come to feek you, be content with the loweft, and take my word for it, that is the beft.

I never was more fatisfied after the Chapters were over, than to find myfelf without any other dignity than the honour of exifting: I then applauded myfelf for having refufed all that they would have

given

given me, and having only myſelf to govern.

The advantage of loving ſtudy, and converſing with the dead, is a thouſand times greater than the frivolous glory of commanding the living. The moſt agreeable command is that of keeping our ſenſes and paſſions in order, and of procuring to the ſoul the ſovereignty which is due to it.

The man who has acquired a habit of application is a ſtranger to the ſpleen; he believes himſelf to be ſtill young, when he is become old; the buſtle of the cloiſter, like the embarraſſments of the world, is always far from him.

I adviſe you then, my dear friend, not only for the good of Religion, not only for the credit of our Order, but ſtill more for your own ſake, to acquire this habit. With a book, a pen, and your thoughts, you will find yourſelf happy, wherever you are—Man has a certain aſylum in his mind as well as in his heart, when he knows how to retire within himſelf.

I am ſenſible of the ſingular confidence

you place in me; and the more fo, as you fhould have applied to the Fathers Colombini, Marzoni, and Martinelli, in preference to me. They are men whofe extenfive knowledge and abilities enable them to give you excellent advice. Adieu! Believe me to be your good friend and fervant.

ROME, 7th June, 1757.

LETTER CIV.

TO R. P***, A MONK OF THE CONGREGATION OF SOMASQUES.

MY MOST REVEREND FATHER,

THE lofs which the Church has fuftained in the perfon of Benedict XIV. is the more affecting to me, as I always found him an excellent Protector. I returned to Rome in the year 1740, which was the firft of his Pontificate, and from that time he never ceafed to honour me with his kindnefs. If you will make his funeral Oration, you have an excellent fubject. You certainly will not forget that

he

he studied among you in the Clementine College, and that there he was initiated into that sublime and extensive knowledge, which made him one of the great Doctors of the Church, and will one day rank him with the Fathers Bernard and Bonaventure.

Take care, in this funeral Oration, that your style rise with the subject, and that the magnanimity which characterised your Hero be expressed with dignity.

Endeavour to be the Historian as well as the Orator, but so as to admit of nothing dry or languid in your recital; for the attention of the Publick should be constantly kept up by some great strokes worthy of the majesty of the Pulpit, and the sublimity of Lambertini.

You will in vain summon all the figures of rhetorick to your assistance, if they do not present themselves of their own accord. Eloquence is only successful when it flows freely from its source, and rises from the greatness of the subject: forced panegyrick is not panegyrick, but amplification.

From the ashes of Benedict XIV. let Virtue spring forth, and seise upon the minds of your Auditors, that they may be transformed into him, and their souls be filled with nothing but the idea of him.

Let there be no trifling detail, no affected phrases, no bombast expressions. Mingle the sublime as much as possible with the temperate, so as to form agreeable shadings, which will adorn your discourse. Be attentive to choose a text which will happily announce the whole plan of your oration, and perfectly characterise your Hero. The division is the touchstone of the Panegyrist, and his discourse cannot be excellent, if that division be not happily chosen.

Scatter moral reflections with discretion, that they may appear to come naturally; that it may be said, they could not be more happily introduced; that *there* was their proper place.

Shun all common-place—and in such a manner, that all may see Lambertini without perceiving the Orator. Praise with delicacy and with moderation, and let your praises soar to Heaven, and remount towards God.

If

If you do not affect the foul by happy furprifes and grand images, your work will only be a work of good fenfe, and you will have made a fimple epitaph, inftead of erecting a maufoleum.

Speak chiefly to the heart, filling it with thofe aweful truths which detach us from the thoughts of this life, and make your Auditors defcend into the tomb of the Holy Father.

Pafs flightly over the infant days of your Hero, for all men are nearly the fame till their reafon begins to fhine forth. Let your periods be neither too long nor too fhort —there can be no ftrength in a disjointed Difcourfe.

Let your Exordium be pompous without bombaft, and your firft fentence announce fomething truely great. I compare the opening of a funeral Oration to the portico of a temple; and I fuppofe the edifice to be beautiful, if I find That majeftick.

In the moft forcible language fhow death overturning Thrones, breaking Sceptres, blafting Crowns, and treading the Tiara under his feet: place the Genius of Benedict

dict upon the ruins, as having nothing to dread from the destroying hand of Time, and defying Death to tarnish his glory, or blot out his name.

Particularise his virtues, and analyse his writings; and every where show the sublimity of his soul, which would have astonished Pagan Rome, as it has edified Christian Rome, and attracted the admiration of the universe.

In a word, thunder and lighten, but manage your clouds so that the light may flash with great splendour, and form the most striking contrasts.

My imagination kindles into flame when I think of so great a Pope as Benedict—that Pontiff regretted even by the Protestants, and whose picture could be drawn only by a Michael Angelo alone.

If I have enlarged upon this article, it is because I know that you can easily catch the spirit of what I recommend to you. A funeral Oration is only excellent as it happens to be picturesque; and strength and truth must guide the pencil.

The generality of elogies descend into the
tomb

tomb with those they praise, because their's is only the eloquence of a day, and the production of fancy, whose lustre is but counterfeit.

It would distract me to see Lambertini celebrated by an Orator who is only elegant: every one should be served according to his taste, and Lambertini's was always unerring, always good.

Engage in it, my dearest friend:—I will most gladly see what you throw out upon paper, being convinced that it will have fire to consume whatever is unworthy of such an elogy. I judge from the productions you have already shown me, and in which I have observed the greatest beauties. It is time that Italy should forget its *concetti*, and assume the masculine and sublime tone of true eloquence.

I endeavour by my advice to form some young Orators, who take the trouble to consult me; and I strive as much as possible to disgust them at those incongruities in our Discourses, which so frequently place the burlesque by the side of the sublime. Strangers startle, and with reason, at so monstrous an alliance. The French especially are unacquainted with this unnatural medley: their Discourses are often superficial, having much less substance than surface; but at least they commonly preserve an equality of style. Nothing can be so shocking as to mount above the clouds, to come afterwards tumbling aukwardly down.

My compliments to our little Father, who would have done wonders, if it had not been for his deplorable state of health.

ROME, 10th May, 1758.

LETTER CV.

TO THE ABBE LAMI.

NO doubt, my dear Abbé, your papers are about to announce the death of our Holy Father. He was a learned man, who has a claim upon all the periodical publications, and to whom all their writers owe the highest encomiums.

He preserved his chearfulness to the last. A few days before his death, when speaking of of a Theatin * whose claim to be placed in the rank of the Saints was under examination, he said, *Great Servant of God, heal me—as you do by me, I will do by you; if you obtain the recovery of my health, I will canonise you.*

The analysis of his works will require such an abridger as you: it would be right to give extracts, that they may pass into the hands of those who have not time to read much, or who cannot purchase them in the great.

Particularly, his book on the *Canonisation of Saints* should be universally known. Besides that he speaks as a physican, a natural philosopher, a civilian, a canonist, and theologian, he there treats on a subject not commonly known.

The Publick imagine, that it is sufficient to send money to Rome to obtain canonisation; while it is notorious that the Pope gets no part of it, and that every possible means is taken to guard against deception on a subject of such importance.

This

* One of the Order of Theatines.

This is so true, that Benedict XIV. whose death we bewail, being Protector of the Faith, begged of two well-informed Englishmen, who were diverting themselves upon the subject of canonisations, to endeavour to shake off all prejudice, and to read with the greatest attention the verbal process which concerned the cause of a Servant of God, who was put on the list of candidates for canonisation.

They consented; and after having read for several days with the most criticising spirit the proofs and testimonies which ascertained sanctity, and all the means which had been employed to come at the truth, they told my Lord Lambertini, that if the same precautions, the same examinations, and the same severity were used with regard to all those that were Canonised, there was no doubt but the matter was pushed *even to demonstration, even to evidence.*

My Lord Lambertini replied: *Well, Gentlemen, notwithstanding what you think, the Congregation rejects these proofs as insufficient; and the cause of the blessed person in question remains undetermined.*

Nothing

Nothing can express their astonishment; and they left Rome perfectly convinced that we do not canonise rashly, and that there are no means easy or difficult left unemployed to come at the truth. The beatification of a Saint is a cause often argued for a whole age; and he who is vulgarly called *l'Avocat du Diable* (the Devil's Counsellor) never fails to collect all the testimonies which can be found to the disadvantage of the Servant of God, and to urge the strongest proofs and most powerful objections to invalidate his sanctity, and lessen the merit of his actions.

There are many reputed Saints who will never be canonised, because there are not sufficient proofs in their favour. It is not sufficient that their virtue has been unstained, or even shining; it must have been heroical, and persevered in till death—*in gradu heroico* (in the highest degree.)

Besides this, the testimony of miracles is required; though unbelievers say, that every thing which is called a miracle is the produce of a troubled mind, or the fruit of superstition;

superstition; as if God Almighty could be chained down by his own laws, without having the power to suspend the execution of them; in which case he would be less powerful than the most petty monarch. But what truths will they not deny, when they are blinded by the corruption of the heart and mind?

God Almighty frequently makes manifest the sanctity of his servants by healing diseases; and if those miracles which are wrought after their death last only for a time, and do not continue for ever, it is because the deity displays himself but seldom, and only to shew that his power is always the same, and that he can glorify his Saints when it seemeth good unto him.

Our Conclave is in labour; and according to custom we cannot know till the last moment who is to be the new Pontiff. Conjectures, wagers, and pasquinades fill the whole town at present—this is an old custom, which will not soon be left off.

As for my part, during the confusion, I am in Rome as if I was not in Rome, wishing only (if it were possible) that Lambertini were

were replaced, and never quitting my cell except for businefs or relaxation. It is there that I enjoy my books and myself, and regale on the reflections of my dear Abbé Lami, to whom I am an unchangeable, and most humble, &c.

Rome 9th May, 1758.

LETTER CVI.

TO THE SAME.

WE have at last got for the Head of the Church Cardinal Rezzonico, Bishop of Padua; who has taken the name of Clement, and will edify the Romans by his piety. It was much against his inclination, and after shedding many tears, that he could be prevailed on to accept it. What a charge for him who would fulfil the duties! He must dedicate himself to God, to all the world, and to himself; he must be solely employed in these great obligations, and have only Heaven in view, amidst the things of this world. His dignity is the more formidable

midable, as he succeeds Benedict XIV. and it will be difficult to appear to advantage after him.

Clement XIII. continues Cardinal Archinto Secretary of State. There could be no better method of being well with Crowned heads, and of making his Pontificate illustrious. He who reigns, must either choose an excellent Minister, or do all himself. Benedict XIII. was the most unhappy of men, from having placed his confidence in Cardinal Coscia; and Benedict XIV. the most happy, by having Cardinal Valenti for his Minister.

It is essential for a Sovereign, but more particularly the Pope, to have good people about him. The understanding of the most clear-sighted Prince is abused, when he allows himself to be dazzled. Then copper is gold in his eyes; and be the consequence what it will, he supports those men he has once patronised.

Discernment is another quality not less necessary to Princes. There is no attempting to impose upon a Monarch who is known to be penetrating; while he who suffers

suffers himself to be led will most certainly be deceived. There are Sovereigns who have done much more hurt by inactivity and weakness, than by wickedness. Men grow weary of doing crying acts of injustice; but are never tired of insensibility and blindness.

The more a Prince is weak, the more he is inclined to be despotick; because authority never destroying itself, is laid hold of by the Ministers, and they become tyrannical.

Another quality which I look upon as essential to good government, is to put every one in his right place. The moral world is directed like a game at Chess, where every thing goes on in order, according to its rank: if we place one pawn in the room of another, the whole is immediately in confusion.

A Sovereign is not only the image of God by the eminence of his rank; he ought to be more so by his understanding. David, although he was but a shepherd, had a superior understanding which directed him,

and

and which he displayed the moment he began to reign.

A Prince who is only good, is no more than what every man ought to be; a Prince who is only severe, has not that love for his subjects which he ought to have.

Alas! how excellently we atoms speak of the duties of royalty! And yet if we were clothed with that dignity, we should not know how to behave ourselves. There is a great difference between speaking and reigning. Nothing resists us when our imagination takes wing, or when we allow our pen to run; but when we see ourselves oppressed with business, surrounded with dangers, beset with false friends, loaded with debts, and chained down to the performance of the most indispensible duties, we lose our courage; we dare not undertake any thing, and by a laziness natural to all men, trust the cares of governing to a subaltern, and only employ ourselves in the pleasures of enjoying and commanding.

One thing is certain, the art of governing is attended with the greatest difficulties. If a Monarch wears an hereditary crown, he has

has a general idea of the greatness of his kingdom, without being able to enter into the *minutiæ* of business, and is easily deceived. If, on the contrary, he comes to an elective crown, he takes on him a sovereignty to which he has not served an apprenticeship, and appears equally embarrassed in the midst of his honours, and in the centre of his business.

He who is placed upon a throne in the decline of life, is fit only to be a representative. He dares not undertake any thing; he is timid, and luke-warm in every thing, especially if he knows not who is to be his successor. This is the situation of the Popes, if they are too old; then they cannot attend to the affairs of Church and State.

But the world will never be without abuses; if they are not in one place, they are in another, because imperfections are the natural inheritance of humanity. *Only in the holy City*, said the great Augustine, *will all be in order, in peace, and in charity; for there shall be the kingdom of God.*

I shall

I shall go and congratulate the new Pontiff, not as a Monk who wants to set himself forward, but in quality of Counsellor of the Holy Office. He does not know me, and I shall not put myself to the trouble of making myself known. I love to remain covered with the dust of my Cloister, and I do not think myself in the least dishonoured.

Adieu! Preserve to us always the good taste of the Medici, and your memory will be long preserved, although you should make it no object of your care.

I am, &c.

Rome, July 5, 1758.

LETTER CVII.

TO A PRELATE.

My Lord,

THE very eminent dignity to which I have been raised by the Sovereign Pontiff has humbled me as much as it would have elated others. I thought I was to have quitted Rome, by the manner in which they announced to me this very extraordinary event, and I have not yet recovered the surprise.

It is a reward conferred in my person on the Order of St. Francis, of which I have the honour to be a member, and I assume nothing of it to myself. My name is only lent on the occasion; for the more I reflect, the more I see, that I had neither on the side of birth, nor on the side of merit, directly nor indirectly, any claim to the Cardinalship.

If any thing can console me in the midst of the trouble with which I am agitated, it is to see myself associated with those illustrious personages who compose the Sacred College, and whose *shoes I am not worthy to untie.* I imagine to myself, that I shall acquire Virtues by communication with theirs; and that by conversing with them, I shall become their copy: we imperceptibly model ourselves by those whose company we frequent. I have declared to my dear Brethren, that I shall never be Cardinal to them, but they will always find me their brother *Laurenca Ganganelli;* especially

as

as I owe to them what I am, and as the habit of St. Francis has procured me the honour of the Purple.

You know me sufficiently to be convinced that I am not dazzled by it. The foul takes no colour, and it is by the foul alone that we can have any value in the fight of God. The Lord, by making us after his own image, and in his likenefs, has given us more than all the dignities of this world can poffibly confer. It is from that view alone I can ever look upon myfelf as great. The Purple, all-dazzling as it is, was not made for my eyes, happily accuftomed to look only towards eternity. That view wonderfully diminifheth worldly grandeur; neither Eminency nor Highnefs can be confidered as any thing in the computation of an immortal life, where nothing appears great but God alone.

I look upon dignities only as fo many more fyllables in an Epitaph, and from whence no fubject for vanity can be extracted; fince he who is interred is beneath even the infcriptions which are read upon his tomb.

Will my ashes have any more feeling by being qualified with the title of Eminency? Or shall I fare better in eternity, when upon earth some feeble voice shall pronounce, or some perishable pen shall write, *Cardinal Ganganelli*.

New dignities are always a new burthen; and more especially the Cardinalate, which imposes a multitude of obligations. There are as many duties to discharge, as there are occasions which require our speaking, without having any respect to aught in this world.

I shall arrange matters so as to be as little affected as possible with this strange metamorphosis. I shall, as usual, remain at the Convent of the Holy Apostles with my dear Brethren, whom I have always tenderly loved, and whose conversation I regard as an inestimable blessing.

If I quit my beloved Cell, where I was happier than all the Kings upon Earth, it is because I must have more room to receive those who come to favour me with their visits: but I shall often say to it, *May my tongue cleave to the roof of my mouth, if ever I for-*
get

get you! I shall frequently go and revisit it, and recollect how many, very many, days passed there like a dream.

Thus I shall make no change in my way of life, and the dear brother Francis shall be to me in place of a whole household; he is strong, he is vigilant, he is zealous, and he will supply all wants. My person is of no greater extent, nor has it grown an atom since my appointment to the Cardinalate, and therefore I do not see that more hands are necessary to serve me.

I walked so well on foot! But what comforts me is, that I shall still continue to walk on foot. I shall allow myself to be dragged in a carriage only when ceremonial requires it, and I shall become Brother Ganganelli again as often as I possibly can. We do not care to quit a way of life we have been accustomed to, especially after having lived fifty-four years in it without any trouble, and in perfect freedom.

I flatter myself that you will come and see, not the Cardinal, but Brother Ganganelli. The first will never be at home to you; but the second shall always be found to repeat to you

you, that whatever station I am in, I shall always be your friend and servant.

Rome, 1 October, 1759.

LETTER CVIII.

TO CONVENTUAL MONK.

My old Friend and Brother,

I Have not yet received the packet you sent me; but I can be patient, though I am naturally very impatient. Our life is nothing but a succession of contradictions and crossings, which we must be able to bear, if we would neither disturb our rest, nor hurt our health.

P. Georgi, always an honour to the Augustines always beloved by those who knew him, has not seen the person you spoke of to me; she passed through the place too quickly for him to obtain that satisfaction. She saw M. Tissot, Procureur-General of the Congregation of the Priests of the Mission, whom I infinitely esteem, because he has great personal merit; because he is a Member

Member of a body who preach to the poor with the greatest succefs; and lastly, because he is a Frenchman.

I must tell you, that I have had a very singular combat with myself since my promotion. Cardinal Ganganelli reproaches Brother Ganganelli for his too great plainnefs; and notwithstanding all the respect which is due to the Purple, the Brother has carried it against the Cardinal. I love to live as I always have lived—poor, retired, and much more with my Brethren than with the Great. It is a matter of taste, for I am very far from ascribing this mode of thinking to virtue.

One thing is certain: I never can put on that cold distant manner, as you would call it, with which persons in office commonly receive people of low extraction who have businefs with them. It is enough for me, if they accost me, or speak to me, to become the equal of my visitors. Is it possible that one human creature should affect haughtnefs towards another, and that a Christian should study his expressions, his gestures, his proceedings, his letters, from the

the dread of appearing too modest with his brethren? Is it possible that any one can refuse an answer to a man, because he has no titles to produce? If the lowest of wretches does me the favour to write to me, I answer him instantly; and I should think myself highly guilty, both in the sight of God and man, if I were to omit that duty. There is no soul despicable in the eyes of Religion and Humanity. There is nothing so pitiful in my eyes, as a great man governed by pride.

I enlarge upon this article to let you know, that the person for whom you are interested may come whenever he pleases, and I shall be entirely his. He will be as well received by Cardinal Corsini, whose politeness corresponds with his noble extraction. If there is a fault in being too affable, it is the fault of the Cardinals. It is rare that you find any haughtiness among them—happily there is not a stranger but does us the justice to declare it.

You will very much oblige me, by telling Signor *Antonio,* when you see him, that

that Cardinal Dataire will not forget his bufinefs.

Take care of your little fhare of health, by watching lefs, walking oftener, and drinking lefs coffee. It is the drink of the ftudious; but it inflames the blood, and then head-achs, fore throats, and pains in the breaft, are felt with more violence. Neverthelefs, I am no enemy to coffee; nor do I think of it like M. Thierry, Phyfician to the Pretender, who lives here, and is of opinion that this liquor is truely a poifon.

Your grand nephew came to fee me on Thurfday: his fpirits are as lively as his eyes. He tore one of my books while playing with it; it is to be hoped, that he will learn to have more refpect for them. He told me with great franknefs, that he would be a Cardinal. I love very much to fee the fouls of children begin to unfold themfelves: it is a bloffom which begins to open, and gives the moft pleafing hopes. He wanted to fay his Breviary with me. Alas! his innocence would have been more agreeable in the fight of God than all my prayers,

I fent

I sent him home by my Chamberlain; but absolutely could not prevail upon him to go till I had given him a chaplet—he told me he would come again to-morrow to have another. Such things are very agreeable in a child only five years old. I wish to God he may one day resemble his father! Adieu! I embrace you in all the fullness of my heart.

Rome, 8th of the Year, 1760.

LETTER CIX.

TO A PROTESTANT MINISTER.

I Am much obliged to you, my dear Sir, for the interest you take in my health. I thank Heaven it is very good, and it would appear to me still better, if I could employ it in something more agreeable to you. The pleasure of obliging should be of all Communions.

I wish with all my soul that I could convince you, that I have all mankind in my heart, that they are all dear to me, and that

that I respect merit wherever it is to be found. If your nephew comes to Rome, as you have taught me to expect, he will find me most zealous to testify to him the affectionate regard I have for you.

My dear Sir, the Church of Rome is so perfectly convinced of the merit of the greatest part of the Ministers of the Protestant Communions, that she would congratulate herself for ever, if she could see them return to her bosom. There would be no occasion to rip up old quarrels of times past, to renew those storms and tempests, when each party, transported by passion, forsook the paths of Christian moderation: but the question would be, how shall we be re-united in the same belief, founded upon Scripture and tradition, such as is handed down to us by the Apostles, the Councils, and the Fathers? No body laments more than I do, the injuries that were done you in the last age: the spirit of persecution is hateful in my eyes.

What

What a multitude of people would not a happy re-union gain! If this could be effected, I would be content to die; for I would sacrifice a thousand lives to be once witness of so happy an event. That moment will come, my dear Sir; because a time must necessarily arrive, when there shall be but one and the same Faith. Even the Jews will enter into the bosom of the Church; and it is in that firm persuasion, founded upon the Holy Scriptures, that they are allowed the full exercise of their religion in the heart of Rome.

God knows, my whole soul is with you, and there is nothing in the world I would not undertake to prove to you, and to all of you, how dear you are to me. We regard the same God as our Father, we believe in the same Mediator, we acknowledge the same doctrines of the Trinity, the Incarnation, and the Redemption, and both of us desire to go to Heaven. It is an established doctrine, that there are not two ways thither: that there should be a centre of unity upon earth, as well as a Chief to represent Jesus Christ. The Church would be truely deformed,

deformed, unworthy of our homage and fidelity, if it were only a body without a head.

The work of the Meſſiah is not like the work of men. What he hath eſtabliſhed, ought to laſt for ever. He has not ceaſed one inſtant to ſupport his Church; and you are too enlightened, my dear Sir, to look upon the Albigenſes as pillars of the truth to which you ought to cleave. Do me the favour to tell all your brethren, all your flock, and all your friends, that Cardinal Ganganelli has nothing ſo much at heart as their happineſs, both in this world and the next; and that he wiſhes to know them all, that he may aſſure them of it. I can add nothing, &c.

ROME, 30th of the Year, 1769.

LET-

LETTER CX.

TO COUNT ***.

I MUST acquaint you, my dear friend, in the folitude where you have been for fome weeks, that Brother Ganganelli, who always tenderly loved you, is become Cardinal, and that he himfelf does not know how, nor wherefore.

There are events in the courfe of human life for which we cannot account; they are brought about by circumftances, and ordained by Providence, which is the origin of all.

However it be, whether in purple or not in purple, I fhall not be lefs in your's than I ever was, but always happy to fee and oblige you.

Sometimes I feel my pulfe, to know if I am really myfelf, being truely aftonifhed that the lot which has elevated me to one of the higheft dignities, did not rather fall upon fome other of my brethren, among whom

whom there are a number whom it would have perfectly suited.

All the world says, when speaking of the new Cardinal Ganganelli, it is incredible that he should arrive at such a rank, without cabal or without intrigue; nevertheless, it is very true.

O my books! O my cell! I know what I have left, but I know not what I shall find. Alas! many troublesome people will come and make me lose my time; many selfish souls will pay me dissembled homage!

For you, my dear Friend, persevere in virtue; being truely virtuous is being superiour to all dignities: perseverance is only promised to those who distrust themselves, and avoid temptations: whoever is presumptuous ought to expect a relapse.

When I think how the publick papers will deign to employ themselves about me, and send my name beyond the Alps, to acquaint different nations when I had the head-ach, or when I was blooded, I

shall

shall smile with contempt. Dignities are snares which have been made splendid, that people might be catched by them. Few know the troubles which attend grandeur; we are no longer our own masters; and let us act how we will, we are sure of having enemies.

I think like St. Gregory of Nazianza, who, when the people ranged themselves on each side to see him pass, thought they imagined him to be some uncommon animal. I own, I cannot accustom myself to this usage; and if this be what is called grandeur, I will most willingly bid it adieu! I look upon all mankind as my brethren, and am delighted when the poor or wretched approach and speak to me.

People will say that my manners are plebeian; but I do not dread that reproach, for I am only afraid of pride. It is so insinuating, that it will do all it can to penetrate and captivate me; but I shall contemplate the nothingness that is in me and around me, and this shall defend me against vanity or self-sufficiency.

Do

Do not think of making compliments when you come to see me; they are a sort of merchandise I do not love, especially from a friend. But here are some visitors, that is to say, every thing which thwarts me, and has rendered me insupportable to myself, for several days. Grandeur has its clouds, its lightenings, and its whirlwinds, like the tempests; I wish for the moment of calm serenity. I am without reserve, and beyond all expression, as before, your affectionate friend and servant, &c.

Rome, 3d October, 1759.

LETTER CXI.

TO CARDINAL CAVALCHINI.

Most Eminent,

YOUR recommendations are commands to me; and I shall not sleep in peace till I have done what you desire. Your Eminency cannot furnish me with too many opportunities of testifying the extent of my esteem

esteem and attachment. In becoming your brother *, I become still more than ever your servant.

It would be proper that we had a particular conference upon what regards the affairs of the Church, as you are infinitely zealous for the good of Religion, which is the only object that ought to engage my attention. We are not Cardinals to impose upon the world by haughtiness, but to be the pillars of the Holy See. Our rank, our habits, our functions, all remind us, that, even to the effusion of our blood, we ought to employ our whole power for the assistance of Religion, according to the will of God and the exigencies of the Church.

When I see Cardinal de Tournon flying to the extremities of the world, to cause the Truth to be preached there in its purity; I find myself inflamed with the noble example, and am disposed to undertake every thing in the same cause.

The Sacred College had always men eminent for their knowledge and zeal, and we should use every effort to renew the example.

* By his rank of Cardinal.

example. Our proceedings ought not to be regulated by human policy, but by the spirit of God; that spirit without which all our actions are barren, but with which we may do all kind of good.

I know your piety, I know your understanding; and I am convinced, that in proper time and place, you can and will speak your mind without any dread.

Some people are endeavouring to make the Holy Father enter into engagements which he may repent of; for, since the death of Cardinal Archinto, there are no longer the same kind of men about him; and the consequences may be unhappy. The Holy See is not respected as it was formerly, and prudence requires that we should pay proper attention to times and circumstances. Jesus Christ, when he recommends to his Apostles *to be harmless as doves*, adds, *and wise as serpents*. An inconsiderate step on the part of Rome, in such critical times as these, may have very bad effects. Benedict XIV. himself, though he was very capable of conciliating people's minds, would have been embarrassed upon this occasion; but he would have been very cautious of infringing the rights of Princes.

What we have to treat about is delicate. Without running counter to the Holy Father or his Council, we must take measures to prevent his being misled by those about him. As his intentions are pure, he does not suspect that he can be imposed on. He ought, at least, to balance the advantages and the disadvantages of what they attempt to make him undertake. We always succeed badly, if we do not calculate beforehand.

The Council affect to give no explanations but to certain Cardinals, and to leave the rest uninformed. The King of Portugal will never change his manner of thinking, and I can see that the other Catholick powers will support and confirm him in his opinions.

Monarchs no longer live detached from one another, as they did formerly; they are all friends, and act with such regard to each other's interests, that if you have the misfortune to offend any one of them, you
will

will offend the whole; and inſtead of having one enemy, you will have all Europe to contend with.

Shall the Holy Father, by an indiſcrete zeal, ſtruggle againſt all the Powers? Shall he fulminate againſt the eldeſt Son of the Church, and againſt his Moſt Faithful Majeſty? He ſhould conſider, that theſe are not Pagan Emperours, whom he would oppoſe, but Catholick Princes like himſelf.

England ſhould have corrected for ever all indiſcrete zeal in the Popes. What would Clement VII. ſay, were he to return upon earth? Would he applaud his work, if he was to ſee that kingdom, which was formerly the nurſery of Saints, become the aſſemblage of all Sectaries, and every kind of error? We ſhould learn to ſacrifice a part, for the preſervation of the whole.

The Holy See can never be more brilliant, never more ſecure, never more in peace, than when it has the Catholick Sovereigns for its defenders and ſupport. It is a harmony abſolutely neceſſary for the glory and good of Religion. The faithful would be expofed to every wind of doctrine, if unfortunately the Princes wanted that deference for the Court of Rome which they ought to have; and the Sovereign Pontiff would fee his flock infenfibly decay, and choofe bad pafture inftead of what he offers them.

The good fhepherd fhould not only call back the fheep that have gone aftray, but labour to the utmoft to prevent any more from wandering. Infidelity, whofe fatal blaft is fpread over all, does not wifh for any thing more than to fee Rome at variance with the kings: but Religion abhors thefe divifions. We fhould not give room for the enemies of the Church to repeat what they have too often faid, that the Court of Rome is intractable, and has a domineering fpirit, which is dangerous to the other States.

The truth is, that every Sovereign is mafter at home, and that no foreign Power has a right to command him. We thought differently in times of trouble and horrour, which it would be dangerous to revive. Charity, Peace, and Moderation, are the

proper

proper arms of Christians, and especially those of Rome, who ought to set an example of patience and humility to all the other Powers of the earth.

We should recollect, that when Peter cut off the ear of Malchus, who was an enemy to Christ, he was reproved by our Saviour, and commanded to put up his sword in the scabbard.

How much more unjustifiable must it then appear, if such a sword was to be employed against those who have always defended, and made it their glory to be the supporters of the Holy See!

There is nothing more dangerous than an indiscrete zeal, which breaks the bruised reed, which extinguisheth the yet-smoking lamp, and which would bring down fire from Heaven.

I know that a Pope is obliged to preserve the immunities of the Holy See; but there is no necessity for embroiling himself with all the Catholic Princes, on account of some seignorial rights.—This would be to stir up the fire of infidelity, and to give pretences for inveighing more than ever against the Church of Rome.

They see badly who see things but in part; the whole should be examined at once, and the consequence of the present proceedings weighed, to judge of the future. *One spark*, said St. James, *will kindle a whole forest*.

Narrow minds imagine, that we wish the destruction of certain Monks, because we will not support them in opposition to the Kings, with whom they are at variance. But besides that more tempests would still follow by resisting those powers, we ought not to give a preference to these Monks, which would embroil the Court of Rome with all the Catholick Princes.

I could not possibly sleep, if I was to wish harm to any one. I sincerely love all the Religious Orders: I desire from my soul that the whole may be preserved; but I reflect upon what is most proper, when it is become necessary to decide. I do not even propose that the Holy Father should dissolve any of them, but that he should at least write to those Crowned Heads, and let them

them know that he will examine the complaints againſt that Order, and then immediately begin to make the enquiry.

Suppoſe Rome expoſed to all theſe potent enemies— how can ſhe ſupport herſelf in the midſt of tempeſts? We are not yet in Heaven; and if God preſerves his Church to the end of Ages, it is by inſpiring thoſe who govern it with a prudence ſuited to times and places, as well as with a love of peace.

It is not to be expected that God will work a miracle to defend an indiſcrete zeal. He leaves ſecond cauſes to act; and when an improper choice is made, things cannot poſſibly go well.

None but the viſionary will refuſe to bend to the exigency of things, when the diſpute neither concerns Faith nor morals. In important affairs we ought always to conſider how they will terminate, if we would avoid the greateſt calamities.

As I know your zeal, my Lord, as well as your underſtanding, I preſume that you will fall upon ſome method capable of ſaving, not the Holy See, which cannot periſh, but

but the Court of Rome, which is expofed to the greateft dangers.

Thefe are my reflections—I perfuade myfelf that you will find them juft. I dare affure you I have weighed them before the Tribunal of God, who trieth the reins and hearts of men, and who knows that I have neither antipathy nor animofity in my heart againft any man.

I have the honour to be, with all the fentiments due to your great underftanding and uncommon virtues,

Your moft humble, &c.

CONVENT of the HOLY APOSTLES,
16th of the Month.

LETTER CXII.

TO CARDINAL S***.

Most Eminent,

I Had not time to speak to you, yesterday, with freedom, upon the great business which at present agitates Europe, and from which Rome will receive a fatal blow, if she does not act with that moderation which Sovereigns require. The Popes are Pilots who are always steering upon tempestuous seas, and consequently are obliged to go sometimes with full sails, and sometimes to furl them, according to circumstances.

Now certainly is the time to employ that wisdom of the serpent recommended by Christ to his Apostles. At a time when Infidelity has broken loose against every Religious Order, it is certainly lamentable to see the Ministers of the Gospel forsaken, who were destined for Colleges, Seminaries, and Miffions, who had diftinguifhed themfelves fo much by their writings upon the truths of our religion; but it remains to be confidered, whether in the fight of God it may be better to engage in a ftrife againft the Powers of the earth, or to relinquifh the fupport of any particular Order of the Church.

For my part, I think, on a view of the ftorm which feems to threaten us on all fides, and may be perceived already hanging over our heads, that it would be more prudent to take the neceffary fteps of ourfelves, and to facrifice any one of our deareft connections, rather than to incur the wrath of Kings, which cannot be too much dreaded.

Let our Holy Father and his Secretary of State regard the Jefuits as much as they will—I fubfcribe with all my heart to their attachment towards that Society, having never had the leaft animofity, nor the leaft antipathy againft any one of the Religious Orders: but I fhall always fay, notwithftanding the veneration which I have for
Saint

Saint Ignatius, and my esteem for those of his Order, that it is extremely dangerous, and even rash, to support the Jesuits, as things are circumstanced at present.

It would undoubtedly be right, that, in quality of Mother and Protectress of all the Religious Orders of the Church, Rome should sollicit in their favour, and employ every means to preserve the Society; provided always that they submit to a reform, according to the Decree of Benedict XIV. and to the desire of all those who sincerely wish well to religion: but my advice is, that when all these means have been tried, the affair should be left in the hands of God and of the Kings.

Rome must always stand in need of the protection and assistance of the Catholick Powers. They are fortresses which shelter her from incursions and hostilities in such a manner, that she never has more glory, nor more authority, than when she seems to yield to these Sovereigns. Then it is that they support her with lustre, and make it their duty to publish every where, and to prove by acts of deference and submission, that they are the tractable sons of the common Father of the Faithful, and that they respect him as the first man in the world, in the eyes of the Faith.

The more I call to mind those unfortunate times when the Popes wandering without help, without asylum, had Emperours and Kings for their enemies, the more I feel the necessity of being at peace with all the Monarchs of the earth. The Church knows but two Orders indispensibly necessary, and founded by Christ himself, to perpetuate his doctrine, and to propagate Christianity, I mean the Bishops and Priests.

The first ages of the Christian world, which we call the best ages of the Church, had neither Monks nor Friars; which evidently proves to us, that if Religion had no need of any but of her ordinary Ministers to preserve her, the Regulars, her auxiliary troops, however useful they may be, are not absolutely necessary.

If the Jesuits have the true spirit of their profession, as I presume they have, they will be be the firſt to ſay, "We will rather ſacrifice ourſelves, than excite troubles and tempeſts."

As a religious Society ought not to depend upon periſhable riches, nor temporal honours, but upon a determined love towards Jeſus Chriſt and his ſpouſe, it ought to retire with the ſame alacrity it was called, if his Vicar, the Miniſter and Interpreter of his will upon earth, ſhould no longer demand its ſervices. The Religious Orders are not reſpectable, indeed ought not to be kept up, but ſo long as they preſerve the true ſpirit of the Church; and as that is always the ſame, independent of all the regular inſtitutions, every Order ought to conſole itſelf, if it happens to be ſuppreſſed.——But frequently vanity perſuades us that we are neceſſary, even at thoſe times when authority judges otherwiſe.

If there was leſs enthuſiaſm, and more ſound principles, every one would agree in theſe truths; and ſo far from raſhly ſupporting a corps which kings complain of, they would induce that ſame corps to retire

retire of itfelf, without murmur or noife; but unfortunately they form an illûfion to themfelves, and imagine that a fingle inftitution cannot be touched, without attacking the very eſſence of religion itfelf.

If in giving up a Religious Order, a dogma was to be altered, a point in morals to be corrupted; it were then, without doubt, better to perifh. But the Church will teach the fame truths after the Jefuits are fupprefſed, which fhe taught before they were eftablifhed—the Church will ftill fubfift: and Chrift will rather raife children to Abraham even from the ftones, to fuftain his work, than leave his myftical body without fuccour or fupport.

The Head of the Church is like the mafter of a magnificent garden, who lops thofe branches at his difcretion, which, by extending too far, may happen to obftruct the view.

Do you, my Lord, who have both zeal and knowledge, confer upon thefe fubjects with the Holy Father. It will be much more proper for you than for me, who confider

sider myself in every respect as the least important Member of the Sacred College. Show his Holiness what an abyss he is digging for himself, when he obstinately resists these Potentates. The rectitude of his heart will make him hearken to you; for we may affirm, that he has taken the resolution of resisting these Powers only because he thinks it to be right. I expect this liberal conduct from your love of the Church, and am

Your Eminency's, &c.

Convent of the Holy Apostles,
9th November, 1768.

LETTER CXIII.

TO A LAY BROTHER.

My dear Brother,

WHY did you hesitate to address yourself to me? Am I another man than I was, because I have the honour of being a Cardinal? My heart and my arms shall always be open to receive

ceive my dear Brethren. I owe them too much ever to forget them; for I owe them every thing.

The confeſſion which you make of your fault, perſuades me that you truely repent of it. However little a man may deviate from the ſtraight path in Cloiſters, he infenſibly gives into exceſs. You have not ſinned through ignorance, and therefore you are more to blame; and what is ſtill worſe, your fault has blazed abroad.

Humble yourſelf before men, and ſhow your contrition before the Throne of Grace, that you may obtain forgiveneſs. I ſhall write to your Superior to receive you again with mildneſs.

My dear brother, you have imagined, that by quitting your retreat you would find infinite ſatisfaction in the world at large. Alas! this world is but a deceiver. It promiſes what it never performs. Viewed at a diſtance it appears to be a parterre of flowers; when nearer ſeen, it proves a brake of thorns.

I pray the Lord that he may touch you feelingly, for every good impulſe comes from

from him. You muft refume your exercifes with the moft lively fervour, and oblige thofe to admire your reformation, who might otherwife reproach you with having gone aftray. You may be fully affured, that you will always be dear to me, and that I fincerely bewail with you the error you have committed. I am your affectionate, &c.

The Card. Ganganelli.

Convent of the Holy Apostles,
18th November, 1760.

LETTER CXIV.

TO R. P. GUARDIAN OF L ***.

IF you have any attachment to me, my Reverend Father, I pray you to receive with cordiality Brother ***, who has fcandaloufly ftrayed from his duty; but he returns, he weeps, and he promifes; and, what is ftill more affecting, Jefus Chrift our model hath taught us how we ought to forgive. I pray you to
look

look upon him who was crucified for the salvation of them that crucified him, and I cannot doubt of obtaining what I desire.

Human nature is so depraved, that I am much less astonished than alarmed at the excesses to which men daily give themselves up. There needs but one emotion of pride, or a selfish regard towards ourselves, to make us lost to grace; and from thenceforth we become capable of every crime.

The more the Lord has preserved us from excesses which require repentance, the more compassionate we ought to be to those who give way to them; for our exemption is the pure effect of his mercy, and for which we should ascribe no merit to ourselves.

Your flock will bless their Pastor, when they see with what tenderness he again receives the stray sheep.

I do not write to you to dispense with the penance prescribed by the Constitutions, but to lighten it as much as is possible, by abstaining from bitter reproaches,

more

more capable of irritating than affecting him.

May your reproof be friendly; may your correction be paternal; may your reception, instead of being austere, have nothing but what is gracious, so as not to terrify the guilty!

Remember that it is always Charity that ought to act; that it is she who ought to punish, and she who should pardon.

I embrace you most sincerely as my former Brother; and I hope to learn even by him whom I recommend to you, that he has found in you rather a father than a master. No body loves or honours you more than

THE CARD. GANGANELLI.

CONVENT of the HOLY APOSTLES,
11th December, 1764.

LETTER CXV.

TO R. P. COLLOZ, PRIOR OF GRAFFENTHAL, AND SUPERIOR-GENERAL OF THE ORDER OF GUILLELMITES.

My Reverend Father,

YOUR letter expresses how much satisfaction you feel on my promotion to the Cardinalship, and of the choice the Holy Father has made of me, among all the Members of the Sacred College, to trust with the protection of your * Order. I did not doubt but your sentiments, in effect, were such; nevertheless, it is a matter of true satisfaction to me, to see the chearfulness which is impressed on your hearts, and to find such certain marks of the confidence with which you honour me. Your Order has certainly been deprived of a great and powerful support by losing Cardinal Guadagni. May the hopes you have conceived of me, restore peace and tranquillity to your souls! At least, I shall employ

*. Every Religious Order has a Cardinal Protector.

employ every effort, my Reverend Father, that you and all your's may find in me a tender friend, a vigilant protector, and a zealous defender of your privileges.

It is with pleafure that I frequently hear the Procureur-General of the Capuchins praifing your Reverence, and thofe of your Order.

Nothing remains to be defired, my Reverend Father, but that you will excufe me for fo long delaying to anfwer you, which was occafioned by my having been oppreffed with a multitude of affairs, that have fcarce left me time to breathe, on a change fo new, and fo little expected on my part. I likewife beg you will put me to the proof, and fee if I can be of any fervice to you. I have had fome converfation with our Holy Father about you:— I fhall fpeak to him on whatever concerns your affairs, every time you choofe to employ me. I beg to recommend myfelf in the ftrongeft manner to the prayers of your Order. I hope to anfwer your Reverence's expectations in fuch a manner, as to convince

vince all of you that you have in me a moft truely affectionate Protector.

I am with all my heart,
My Rev. Father, &c.

ROME, CONVENT of the HOLY APOSTLES,
20th May, 1769.

LETTER CXVI.

TO THE ABBE F***.

IT is eafy to obferve, both in your writings and converfation, my dear Abbé, that you do not read the Fathers of the Church fo much as you ought. Do you know that they are the foul of Chriftian eloquence, and that like thofe fertile trees which at once form the ornament and riches of a garden, they produce abundance both of flowers and of fruits?

The Church is proud of producing their works as fo many monuments of victories which fhe has gained over her enemies, and every enlightened Chriftian ought to be delighted with reading them. The more they are examined, they will be found the more

more conspicuously bright—every Father of the Church has a characteristical distinction. The genius of Tertullian may be compared to iron, which breaks the hardest bodies, and will not bend; St. Athanasius to the diamond, which can neither be deprived of its lustre nor solidity; St. Cyprian to steel, which cuts to the quick; St. Chrysostome to gold, whose value is equal to its beauty; St. Leo to those ensigns of dignity which are at once graceful and majestick; St. Jerome to brass, which neither dreads swords nor arrows; St. Ambrose to silver, which is solid and shining; St. Gregory to a mirrour, in which every one sees himself; St. Augustine to himself, as singular in his kind, though universal.

As to St. Bernard, the last of the Fathers in the Order of Chronology, I compare him to those flowers of the velvet kind, which shed an exquisite perfume.

If the French reckon Bossuet, Bishop of Meaux, among the Fathers, it is a premature judgement, which cannot be submitted to, until the universal Church has pronounced

pronounced it, as she has the sole right of assigning the rank which is due to Writers. Even St. Thomas Aquinas has not obtained the title of a Father of the Church; and it is not to be presumed that the Doctors who have succeeded him, should enjoy that prerogative: but every nation has an enthusiasm for its own Authours; yet it must be allowed, that the Bishop of Meaux was a burning and shining lamp, whose light can never be obscured.

I confess to you, my dear Abbé, if I know any thing, I owe it to the reading the Fathers, especially the works of St. Augustine. Nothing escapes his sagacity; nothing is beyond his depth, nothing above his sublimity; he contracts, he extends himself, he walks in a path of his own, varying his style and manner according to the subjects which he treats of, and always with the same advantage, always elevating the soul, even into the bosom of God; a sanctuary of which he seems to hold the key, and where he seems imperceptibly to introduce those whom he nourisheth with his sublime ideas. I particularly admire him upon the

subject

subject of Grace. I wish to Heaven, that his doctrine upon that point had been established in all the Schools, and all minds! Presumptuous writers would not then have endeavoured to found an impenetrable abyss, the grace of Jesus Christ would have preserved all its rights, and man his liberty.

What afflicts me is, that the Fathers of the Church are scarcely read; and they who have occasion to consult them, trust to extracts, which are often unfaithful, and always too much abridged. A Priest or a Bishop made it his duty formerly to read the Fathers of the Church, as much as to say his breviary; but now-a-days they are only known by name, except it be in the Cloisters, where that excellent custom is not quite left off: whence it comes, that in many countries they have meagre Theologians, without life or soul; students who can only syllogise; and instructions which contain nothing but words without meaning.

Nevertheless, I ought to say to the praise of the Sacred College, without meaning to compliment

compliment it, that they have always had members who have perfevered in the ftudy of the Fathers; and fome may be named who actually prefer that kind of reading to all other employment.—Our Schools likewife feel that influence, where they teach only the doctrine of St. Auguftine and St. Thomas—a certain means of avoiding whatever breathes novelty.

Let me conjure you, then, to lay it down as a rule, to read the Fathers every day; it requires but a beginning; for when once you enter upon them, you will not care to leave them—they are always with God, and they will place you on the fame feat with themfelves, if you nourifh yourfelf daily with their writings.—It is reading the Holy Scripture to read them, for they explain it in a mafterly manner, and quote it on all occafions.

It were to deprive me of three-fourths of my exiftence, if the confolation of entertaining myfelf with the HolyFathers was taken from me—the more they are prefent, the more I am comforted, the more I rejoice, and the greater I think myfelf.

Profit by my leffons, and you will love me if you love yourfelf; for in reading the Fathers, you will make acquifitions a thoufand times more precious than weath or titles. An ecclefiaftick has nothing to do with the world, but to inftruct and edify it. I am with all my heart, and with the warmeft defire to fee your talents produce good fruit,
Your affectionate,
THE CARD. GANGANELLI.

ROME, 13th December, 1768.

LETTER CXVII.

TO R. P***, HIS FRIEND.

YOU have given me a fingular pleafure, by not mentioning that I had written to you. Without being myfterious, I am a great friend to difcretion; and although I have been eight-and-twenty years in the Convent of the Holy Apoftles, I never acquainted my brethren with what connections I have.—They may guefs, if
they

they will, or if they can; but they know nothing: *secretum meum mihi*—My secret is my own.

I lately saw the Cardinals York, Porsini, and John Francis Albani, whose excellent qualities I highly esteem; but I have learned nothing from them of what I wanted to know.

I subscribe with the greatest pleasure to all the obliging things you say of the Prelate Durini: he has joined the Italian sagacity to the pleasing manners of the French, and deserves to attain the greatest dignities.

I have learned nothing of the late resolutions of the great Personage you speak of; I see him but very seldom, and in a most reserved manner—he does not believe me to be his friend. Is he wrong? Is he right? This is what he himself cannot decide, notwithstanding all the *finesse* he is supposed to be master of; but most certainly, God knows, I bear no ill will to him, because I never have done so to any one.

I will

I will recommend the good work which you mention to the Cardinals Fantuzzi and Borromeo, who breathe nothing but charity. Do you yourself deliver the enclosed, which I send you for M***, and let me have his answer by the flying Post, which is both quick and sure. For some time past my correspondences overpower me, and yet I cannot get rid of them. From this time do not lose half a page in showing me respect: I wish you to write to me as to Brother Ganganelli. I am always the same individual, whatever efforts may be made use of to persuade me to the contrary; for, alas! if I was to attend to *etiquettes* and flatterers, they would intoxicate me with their ridiculous incense.

I love to be simply myself, and not to be beset with all the accompaniments of grandeur: Your great littlenesses disgust me; and surely they who are fond of them, must have but a contemptible spirit.

There is no probability that our common friend can recover; he has a complication of disorders, any one of which is sufficient to destroy the strongest person.

I am

I am folliciting a place which I think will fuit your nephew, provided he can bear confinement, and hear grumbling; for the nobleman, whofe Secretary I intend him to be, has the unfortunate madnefs of falling in a paffion at every trifle: but his heart is not the lefs excellent—it is a blot which fhould be overlooked, becaufe of his goodnefs. He is like Benedict XIV. who always concluded by beftowing fome favour upon thofe he had fcolded. You fee that I am in a humour to prate, and that I have not the air of a man of bufinefs. When I have faid my breviary, and finifhed my engagements, I chat more than is perhaps liked, but then I have need of it.

I leave you with yourfelf, that is to fay, in the beft company that I know; and am, as ufual, and for my whole life,

Your affectionate fervant,

THE CARD. GANGANELLI.

ROME, 6th December, 1768.

LETTER CXVIII.

TO M. D***.

THE giving of alms is not sufficient to please God, for charity extends over all; you should not oppress your tenants, nor molest your vassals; they who with the greatest severity exact trifles which they ought to despise, have not a proper sense of Religion. Christianity is unacquainted with that sordid interest which is attentive to little things; and they have only the bark who are always upon the watch with their tenants, for fear of being cheated. The heart is become too earthly, when it is over-anxious about worldly matters.

Why torment yourself, Sir, so solicitously about the things that perish? The kingdom of Jesus Christ should have worshippers in spirit and in truth, whose hearts are not contracted by a self-interested conduct, and views merely carnal.

I am mortified when I see people of fortune living in dread of want, and though very rich, often much more attached to a dirty piece of gold than a poor labourer would be.

I dare add, Sir, that all your works of devotion will be absolutely useless, if you do not detach yourself entirely from the things of this world; and cease to be the tyrant of your debtors, by a greediness after riches. It is better to forego a right, than to recover it by oppression. The spirit of justice which you plead in your favour, has no connection with continual distrust, with apprehensions about future want, and with eternal wranglings.

If there are some disputes between you and your tenants, settle them more to their advantage than your own; it is conformable to the advice of Jesus Christ, who orders us, if they ask our cloak to give our coat also. All your superfluities, and even a part of your necessaries, on urgent occasions, belong to the poor; so that you will be guilty if you accumulate. These are harsh truths, but the Law was not made by me.

The

The affair you spoke to me about, could not be in better hands than M. Braschi's: his rectitude is equal to his understanding, and there is no fear of his being prejudiced: nevertheless, if you desire it, I will speak a few words to him,

I am, Sir,
With the sentiments due to you, &c.
THE CARD. GANGANELLI.
Rome, 21st of the present Month.

LETTER CXIX.
TO MY LORD ***.

I Have not been accustomed to see such a genius as your's become the dupe of modern philosophy. Your understanding should set you above the sophistry which the fashionable principles engender, and which levels us to the sad condition of the brutes.

If there is a God, as Nature cries aloud through all her works, there must be a Religion. If there is a Religion, it must be incomprehensible, sublime, and as ancient as the world, as being an emanation from an infinite and eternal Being. If thefe are its characters, it muft be Chriftianity; and if it is Chriftianity, it muft be acknowleged to be divine, and heart and foul fhould acquiefce in it.

Is it then credible that God Almighty fhould difplay this Univerfe in fuch fplendour, only to feed the eyes of flocks of men and beafts, that ought to be confounded together, as having all the fame deftiny; and that this intelligence which dwells in us, which combines, which calculates, which extends beyond the earth, which mounts above the firmament, which recollects the ages paft, and penetrates into thofe which are to come, and has an idea of that which is to laft for ever, fhould fhine forth one moment, only to be diffipated afterwards like a feeble vapour?

What is that voice which inceffantly proclaims within you, that you were born for great things? What are thofe defires which continually renew themfelves, and which make you feel that there is nothing in this world capable of occupying the wifhes of your heart?

When

When man eftrangeth himfelf from God, he is like a diftempered wretch rolling in agony; and the light of his reafon, which he extinguifheth, leaves him in the midft of a darknefs replete with horrour.

The fame truth which affures you of your own exiftence; I would fay that intimate teftimony which you find within yourfelf, affures you of the exiftence of a God, and cannot give you a lively idea of him, without impreffing you with an idea of Religion. The worfhip which we render to the Supreme Being, is fo linked with him, that our heart is not fatisfied but when it is rendering homage to him, or conforming to the order which he hath eftablifhed.

If there is a God, he ought naturally to be beneficent; and if he is beneficent, you ought by the jufteft confequence to thank him for his benefits. Neither your exiftence nor your health comes from yourfelf: about feven-and-twenty years ago, you was nothing, when all on a fudden you became an organifed body, enriched with a foul to act as mafter, to command and guide your frame according to its will and pleafure.

This reflection engages you to seek for the Authour of life; and when you will examine, you will find him in yourself, and in every thing which surrounds you, without any one of these objects being able to boast of their being a part of his substance; for God is single and indivisible, and cannot therefore be identified with the elements.

If the Religion which he hath established hath taken different forms, and has been since perfected by the coming of the Messiah; it is because God hath treated it as he has done our reason, which at first was only a feeble ray; but, afterwards, disclosing itself by degrees, at last appears in the brightest light.

Besides, is it for man to interrogate the Deity with regard to his conduct? Is it for a creature to regulate the ways of his Creator, and to prescribe a manner of operating to him? God communicates himself to us in part, but still reserves to himself the right of absolute dominion, because there is nothing but what is truely subject to him. If he clearly manifested his designs to us here below, if the mysteries which astonish and confound us were laid open to our view, we should have that intuitive sight which he reserves till after this life, and death would then be unnecessary. Evidence is only for Heaven, *cognoscam, sicut & cognitus sum* *: yet we would anticipate that moment, without reflecting that every thing is regulated by Infinite Wisdom, and that we have nothing to do on our part, but to submit and to adore. The unbeliever changes nothing of the designs of God, when he dares to rise up against him. He even enters into his plan, that comprehensive plan where the evil concurs with the good for the harmony of this world, and for the happiness of the next.

Religion and nature are equally derived from God; and both the one and the other, though in different manners, have their mysteries and their incomprehensibilities; and by the same reason that the existence

of

* I shall know God, as I am known by him.

of nature is not denied, though its operations are often concealed, Religion cannot, nor ought not to be rejected, on account of its obscurities.

There is nothing here which hath not a dark side; because our soul, weighed down by a body which oppresses and darkens it, is not capable of seeing every thing. It is in a kind of infancy here below, and should have light in proportion to the weakness of its sight, till death disengages it from the oppressive load which weighs it down. It is like a tender bird which pants and cries in its nest, till it can spring up into the air, and take its natural flight.

The progress of Religion is admirable in the eyes of a true Philosopher. It is at first seen like a twilight issuing from the bosom of Chaos; then like Aurora it announces the day; which at last appears, but surrounded with clouds, and cannot manifest itself in meridian brightness, until the Heavens shall be opened.

Hath then the unprincipled unbeliever any thing in particular which tells him, that
what

what we believe is chimerical? At what time, and in what place has this secret light come to shine upon him? Is it in that moment when his passions ingulf and govern him? Or is it in the midst of public shows and pleasures, where he commonly passes his life?

It is astonishing, my Lord, how men give up all the authority of tradition, and elude all the strength of the greatest testimonies, to refer blindly to two or three people who give them lessons of infidelity. They will not allow of inspiration, yet they look on those people as oracles; from whence it may be easily concluded, that nothing but their passions can attach them to infidelity. They abhor a Religion which restrains them when they would follow the torrent of their vices, and swim in the midst of the waves of a world agitated with foaming billows.

Christianity is a superb picture traced out by the hand of God, and which he presented to man while it was yet but sketched, till the moment Jesus Christ came to finish it, waiting the time when he should give it the lustre and colouring it is to bear throughout eternity.

Then Religion will be the only object to engage our attention, because it will be then the essence of God himself, making, as St. Augustine expresseth it, *a whole with him*.

This progress is conformable to that of the time which constitutes this life, and which does not exist but by succession. God has thus varied the forms of Religion, because we are in a variable world; but he will fix it unalterably in Heaven, because there no change will be known. These are the combinations and proportions which display the wisdom of the Supreme Being. Religion being formed for man, it was his pleasure that it should follow the progress made by man, according to the different modes of his existence.

They who are intent upon this world, see nothing of all this; but you would judge of these things as I do, if you were disengaged from all the pleasures and all the riches which make you a Materialist,

in

in spite of yourself. Christianity is spirit and life; and they stray widely from it, who are occupied only about what is corporeal. Souls become enlightened at death, only because they are no longer weighed down by bodies which immure and darken them. True philosophy, by disengaging man from whatever is carnal, does what death will finally effect; but it is not the modern philosophy, which acknowledges no existence but that of matter, and looks upon metaphysicks as a science purely chimerical, although much more certain than Natural Philosophy, which has only its existence in the senses.

I do not enter into the proofs of Religion, because they have been so often and so well explained already in immortal works that I could only repeat them. Jesus Christ is the beginning and the end of all things, the key of all the mysteries of grace and nature; so that it is by no means surprising that we should wander after a thousand absurd systems, when we do not steer
by

by that sublime Compass. If you do not admit of Jesus Christ, I must say as Cardinal Bembo did to a Philosopher of his time, *I cannot give you a reason for any thing in Natural or Moral Philosophy.* Even the creation of this world is inexplicable, incomprehensible, and impossible, if it was not effected by the Incarnate Word; for God can have no other intention in what he does, but what is infinite. This is the reason why St. John called our Saviour *Alpha and Omega*; and that the Apostle told us that the ages were made by him: *Per quem fecit et sæcula.*

Study, then, as much as a creature is capable, this Man-God, and you will find all the treasures of science and wisdom in him; you will observe, that he is the first link of that chain which bindeth all things visible and invisible; and you will acknowledge him to be that divine breath which inspires justice and holiness into all hearts.

The unbeliever can never give a satisfactory answer, when you ask him, Who is this

this Jesus Christ, this man at the same time so simple and so divine, so sublime and so humble, so pure in the whole course of his life, so great in the moment of his passion, so magnanimious at his death? But to answer this question without evasion. If he is only a man, he is an Impostor; for he hath said he was God; and from that time, what becomes of his sublime virtues? what becomes of his Gospel, in which he forbids the use of the least equivocation? and how account for his Disciples victories in all parts of the world? And if he is a God, what ought we to think of his Religion, and those who dare to combat it?

Ah! my Lord, behold what is better to know, and better to examine, than all the profane sciences which you study. Sciences will be at an end; *Linguæ cessabunt, scientia destruetur* *; and nothing will remain but the knowledge of Jesus Christ, which will ride triumphant upon the abyss, when time and the elements shall be swallowed up.

* Languages shall cease, and Science be destroyed.

Consider

Consider only yourself, and that view will necessarily lead you to truth. The smallest motion of your finger declares the action of God upon your body; this action announces a Providence; this Providence informs you that you are dear to your Creator; and this information leads you from truth to truth, till you come to those which are revealed.

If you are neither the creator of yourself, nor your own ultimate end, you ought necessarily to search for Him in whom these two qualities subsist. And what can that be, if it is not God?

Religion will be always sure to gain her cause in the eyes of all those who have settled principles. To come at the truth, it is sufficient to remount to its source, to analyse and investigate the ends of its institution: but the wicked dishonour and disfigure it, and substitute a skeleton in its place. I am not surprised, then, that they who are not instructed, and who put their trust in the false philosophy of the age, should look upon it as a bug-bear.

My

My Lord, I expect from the rectitude of your soul, and the extensive powers of your mind, a more solid judgement than what you have hitherto formed with regard to Christianity. Shake off all these systems, and all the opinions with which you have been unfortunately biassed; enter like a new man into the way which tradition will open to you, and you will judge very differently; appeal from your prejudices to yourself; for as yet you yourself have not pronounced any opinion upon this subject. As for my part, I say what my heart and soul dictate to me, when I assure you of all the affection with which I shall remain, during life,

Your servant, &c.
The CARD. GANGANELLI.

ROME, 29th Nov. 1768.

LETTER CXX.

TO COUNT ***.

THE reflections which you have made upon the present state of the different Courts of Europe are very judicious. It is plain that you know them perfectly; and though you are not of their cabinets, you are very well acquainted with what is passing there.

It is well to be on a level with the Age, to know it perfectly, and to observe the springs which move the great personages who figure on the stage of life.

The person you speak of *is a man of wool*, without consistence or steadiness, and upon whom, consequently, there can be no dependence. There is another person you know, zealous as he ought to be for the August House of Bourbon; but though he leaves his Palace with a firm resolution to speak strongly to the Holy Father about the affair of Parma, he is scarcely got into

his

his prefence, when awe ftrikes him dumb. As to the little Prelate who fhould act and conftitute himfelf Mediator, he is an indecifive perfon, who is always putting off every thing till the morrow, and who has no other anfwer but *Vederemo,* We fhall fee.

We might eafily fpeak about it to the General of ***; but it is not fafe to confide in him at prefent; efpecially when even the fecret enjoined by the Holy Office is not kept. As to his Affiftant, he is merely a well-meaning man.

Many of the great men here are with reafon attached to France and Spain; but they dare not explain themfelves, they are fo teized and befet by numbers, who make Heaven fpeak as they pleafe.

A devotion faintly enlightened, which is unhappily but too common, is conftantly whifpering, that all fhould be facrificed to defend the interefts of God; as if God required that his Firft Minifter upon Earth fhould embroil himfelf with all the Catholick Powers to fupport fome feignorial rights;

rights; and, at all adventures, to preserve a Corps, which can be of no further utility, when the tide of prejudice runs against it.

Let us suppose, for a moment, that there is nothing against them but prejudice; still it is certain, that they can be no longer useful, when opposed by powerful Princes; but it is impossible to make people hear reason upon this subject, who have adopted a certain manner of thinking.

All this forms a labyrinth, from whence we can see no exit; and the best way we can take is to be silent, and wait God's good time. When he pleases, he can enlighten their minds, and make them know his intentions.

The evil is, that the longer they are kept in suspence, the more they are enflamed. I am persuaded, Monf. the Count, notwithstanding all the talents which I know you possessed of, that you do not see an easy means of extricating us out of this confusion. We have to do with people who loudly exclaim against all propositions of accommoaccomodation; and it is impossible to say anything to them, because they fancy themselves to be inspired.

Nevertheless, I cannot help being greatly offended at some discourse that certain persons hold against Clement XIII. especially as it is not permitted to speak against the High Priest; and we read in the Epistle of St. Jude, that St. Michael durst not utter curses even against the Devil, but was content to say, The Lord rebuke thee: *Non est ausus judicium inferre blasphemiæ, sed dixit: Imperet tibi Dominus.*

From hence I conclude, that the generality of men, be their manner of thinking what it will, bend Religion to their prejudices. Some are great friends to the Religious Society which is the subject of the present disputes, while others are equally its enemies; and the consequence is, that things are not seen as they ought to be, and that truth can no longer be heard amidst the clamours of passion. For my part, who always kept in the middle between the two extremes of parties, and detest

detest cabals and prejudices, I think that the Pope can do nothing better, than under the guidance of God to examine all the papers both for and against them, as likewise all the inconveniencies which result either on the one side or the other, and then he can and ought to pronounce, for he is judge; and I never pretended that he was the simple Minister of the will of Princes. None but he who established a Religious Order can destroy it; but he has so clear a right, that it would be madness to dispute it with him.

What comforts me amidst all these evils, is, that though the bark of St. Peter must always be agitated, the Lord likewise will support it, even in the midst of the greatest tempests. You are surely more persuaded of these things than any man; you, Sir, who have always made eternal truths the object of your meditations, and have seen whatever has any relation to Religion with the eyes of the Faith. These eyes, far different from those of Philosophy, raise us above this world, and give us us to range in the divine immenfity. There can be nothing, therefore, fo abfurd, as to fay, with the modern Philofophers, that the views of Chriftians are extremely limited. Can a foul be contracted in its ideas when it extends its thoughts even to Eternity, and, rifing above the Univerfe, approaches to God himfelf, a pure and immaterial Spirit?

In drawing a parallel between Religion and Philofophy, it will be immediately perceived, that the former gives a boundlefs extent to all the faculties of the foul; and that the latter contracts them within a very narrow circle. This world is the *ne plus ultra* of the Philofophers of the prefent times; but with the Chriftian, 'tis only an atom. The one makes it his happinefs and his end; the other looks upon it merely as a fhadow which paffeth away, and regardeth it only with a glance of his eye. This adores it, becaufe it is his all and his God; That looks upon it as a vapour, which will very foon be difpelled.

Do not reckon upon the Prelate***; he is too bufy.

If any change happens here, I fhall be ready to acquaint you with it. But there muft be a terrible concuffion for that to take place. I have the honour to be, Monf. the Count, &c.

My Compliments to M. the Abbé.

LETTER CXXI.

TO A PRELATE.

YOU have very fenfibly obliged me by the fervices you have done the Reverend Father Aimé de Lambale. He is a Capuchin for whom I entertain a fingular regard, on account of his good qualities. He has the virtues of his profeffion; that is to fay, he is humble, gentle, zealous, and gives great application to preferve the rules of his Order in their full force.

I expect your return with impatience, efpecially as the fubject of our converfation
will

will be fome people's readinefs to talk, and backwardnefs to execute.

Every day brings us fome very extraordinary news, which the next day contradicts. When the fpirits are in a ferment, and affairs of confequence are in agitation, every one fets up for a politician and news-monger; efpecially in Rome, where we have fo many idle fpeculators.

Some have fears, others have hopes, this life being only a fucceffion of difquiets and defires. It was given out yefterday, that the King of Naples had marched fome of his troops into our neighbourhood.

St. Ignatius who was inflamed with zeal for the glory of God, did not forefee the ftrife which would one day be occafioned by his children. It is faid, however, that he begged of God they might always be fufferers. If that be the cafe, he has certainly been heard; for it muft be allowed, that for fome time they have undergone a number of calamities. I have really been exceedingly affected by their misfortunes—

they are my brethren, by the double title of Men and Monks: *and if thefe things are done in the green tree, what will be done in the dry?—Quid in arido fiet?*

You will no longer find your Director here. We have buried him. This fame Death, who generally comes without being called, gives us no refpite. He goes his rounds day and nigh, and yet we live in as much fecurity as if we thought he would never come near us.

I flatter myfelf that you will bring me the little picture which I requefted of you. Depend upon my efteem and friendfhip: it is all that I can give you, but I give it amply, being, &c.

Rome 23d April, 1768.

LETTER CXXII.

TO THE MARQUIS OF CARACCIOLI.

SIR,

I Return you a thousand thanks for the book you was so obliging as to send me, and which has for its Title *Les Derniers Adieux de la Marechale à ses Enfans:* It is sentimental, and makes such lively impressions upon the heart, that I was very deeply affected with it. You should give it to us in Italian; and the rather, as I look upon it to be a complete treatise on education.

I am sorry that you was not provided in time with all the interesting anecdotes of Benedict XIV. You were too late in setting about that work. When it is intended to publish the history of a Sovereign Pontiff, memoirs should be collected during his life: every one is then eager to furnish them; but after his death he is immediately forgotten, and frequently even by those men who are indebted to him for their fortunes.

Your literary purfuits are fo beneficial to the Publick, that I advife you to continue them, provided they be not injurious to your health.—Believe me to be, more than I can exprefs,

    Your affectionate fervant,
     THE CARD. GANGANELLI.

ROME, 13th September, 1768.

LETTER CXXIII.

TO THE AMBASSADOR OF ***.

IF the affairs of Parma, like that of the Jefuits, were connected with the Faith, there could be no temporifing, accommodation, nor capitulation; becaufe the anfwer from the Popes to him who would change his Faith, is, *You muft rather die.*

One thing only is certain, I am afraid that the Kings will at laft do juft what they pleafe, and that we fhall be forced to yield at a moment when all fubmiffion may be rejected.

       Thofe

Those times are now no more, when men of all ranks brought to Rome their vows and their offerings; yet, were she still in the same situation, could she conscientiously infringe upon the rights of Kings? A Pope ought undoubtedly to preserve all his immunities; but not so tenaciously as to hazard so dangerous a schism.—Nothing is so much to be guarded against as dividing the body of Christ's Church.—Rome is the centre of unity, and therefore ought not, for the sake of articles which neither affect Morals nor the tenets of Religion, to provoke those who live in her bosom to separate from her Communion.

If, when the Kings began to complain of the Jesuits, the General himself had written to those Monarchs to soften their anger, and to desire that the offenders might be severely punished—if the Holy Father himself had followed this plan, the Crowned Heads might have been appeased; and I really think this affair might have been brought to a happy issue, provided a reformation had been offered. But they were obstinate, and still persist with the same pertinacity to support the Society:

and this is what stirs up so many people against them.

P. Pontalti, General of the Carmelites, acted like an excellent Politician, when he wrote to the King of Portugal to beg that he would prevent his Monks from trading to Brazil. He advised R. P. Ricci to take the same step; but that Father would not listen to his counsel.

Where is the Sovereign who may not, in his own kingdom, either protect or expel such as offend him? I dare say, that the acting Minister did not take this affair rightly, and did not foresee all its consequences: *there are fine eyes that see nothing.*

The example of Avignon, Benevento, and Porte-Corvo, shows us, that if there is not an immediate accommodation, some other places will be seised; and thus insensibly we shall lose territories to which long possession had given us an indubitable right.

Benedict XIV. though timid, would have satisfied the Kings in this crisis; and it is unfortunate that things are seen in a different light by Clement XIII. whose piety

piety we respect, as well as that of the Cardinal his nephew. I ventured to speak to him on that subject, and he was struck with what I said; but some people, who were interested in keeping up the opinions which they had suggested to him, immediately interposed, and gave him some specious reasons for persisting in his sentiments. They said, that a Religious Order which had done the greatest services in both Worlds, and had made an express vow of obedience to the Holy See, ought absolutely to be preserved; and that the attempt to destroy it originated solely from a hatred to Religion. But they did not tell him, that, as the common Father of the Faithful, he ought not to provoke the Princes who were most distinguished for their religion and obedience to the Holy See; nor did they tell him what might be the result of a schism between that See and Portugal; and that the Head of the Church should tremble, when a separation is threatened which may have the most fatal consequences.

The loss of a small proportion of territory, is nothing in comparison with the souls which may be lost by a schism. What a lesson would England afford to Clement VII. if he was alive at this day! It makes one shudder with horrour. Certainly the Sovereigns who reign at present will never think of a separation; but can we answer for those who are to succeed them? Those measures which are apparently most pious, are not always most expedient.—A Pope is established the Head of the Church, that he may root out as well as plant. The valuable books which the Jesuits have left us will live after them. The Religious Orders have not been gifted with infallibility nor *indefectibility:* if they were all to be abolished this day, the loss would be undoubtedly great; but the Church of Jesus Christ would neither be less holy, less Apostolical, nor less respectable. The Religious Societies are upon the footing of auxiliary troops; and the great Pastor is only to form a judgement when they are useful, and when they are no longer so.

The

The Humiliars, and even the Templars, did good for a time, becaufe there has been no Order but what has edified, efpecially at the beginning of its inftitution; yet they were fuppreffed when the Kings and Popes found it neceffary.

Certainly I muft regret the good which the Jefuits might have done; but I fhould much more regret the Kingdoms that might have feparated from us on their account.—Thefe Fathers themfelves ought to feel the juftnefs of my reafonings; and I have the prefumption to believe, that I could make them acknowledge it, if I had a conference with them, and they would fhake off the prejudices which are attached to all conditions of life. If my friend P. Timoné had been their General, they might probably have ftill fubfifted.

This is my way of thinking, though of a Religious Order myfelf; and I would confent to the diffolution of my own Society, if (which God forbid!) it fhould become obnoxious to the refentment of the Catholick Princes.

Happily, there are fome devotional fantafms by which I have never been dazzled.

I weigh

I weigh events according to Religion and equity; and as thefe are two certain lights, I fhall ever be determined by their direction.

If there were no other intereft in the Church but that of Jefus Chrift, all the Faithful would wait in peace for the events marked out by Providence, without engaging warmly either for Cephas or Apollos. But we are only guided by fenfible affections; and becaufe we have once known a Monk who has edified by his conduct, and all whofe inftructions have been excellent, muft we therefore conclude that we neither can, nor ought to fupprefs the Order of which he was a member?—Is this to reafon, or to judge?

When we have neither feen the informations nor the arguments upon which we fhould frame a judgement, an attempt to pafs fentence is abfurd. Here is a great conteft between Kings and a Religious Order eminent for its talents and credit:— when we do not know the motives from which they act, we neither can nor ought to to pronounce an opinion. I say once more, that I do not assert that the Jesuits ought to be suppressed, but I think the complaints of the Kings should be attended to; and if there are strong reasons for it, that then the Order should be abolished.

To this day we know not precisely the reasons for the destruction of the Templars, and yet there are people who already pretend to be acquainted with the motives for the suppression of the Jesuits. I wish with all my heart that they may be able to justify themselves, and that there may be neither division nor dissolution; for I have a soul truely pacifick, and incapable of hating any one, more particularly a Religious Order.

    I have the honour to be, &c.

ROME, 29th October, 1768.

LETTER CXXIV.

TO THE MARQUIS OF ***.

WE are now in the moſt critical ſituation the Court of Rome was ever engaged in! All Europe thundering againſt us, and unfortunately we have nothing to oppoſe to this raging tempeſt. The Pope truſts in Providence; but God Almighty does not work miracles every time he is called upon; nor can we expect that he will interpoſe his power, merely that Rome may maintain a right of ſeignory over the Duchy of Parma.

In the Roman Catholick Kingdoms, Rome has no adminiſtration but what is purely ſpiritual; it is only in the Eccleſiaſtical State that ſhe has any temporal authority; and ſhe is even indebted for that to the conceſſion of thoſe Sovereigns whom we are ſollicited to oppoſe.

The Court of Rome cannot forget that ſhe owes almoſt all her riches and ſplendour to France; and if ſhe does remember it, how can ſhe avoid compliance with the deſire fire of Louis XV. especially as he only asks those things which he has a right to exact?

I compare the four Kingdoms that principally support the Holy See, to the Cardinal Virtues; France to Strength, Spain to Temperance, &c.

The Holy See thus defended, shows herself formidable to her enemies, and then may we say, *Cadent à latere tuo mille, et decem millia à dextris tuis; ad te autem non appropinquabit**.

I own to you, my dear Sir, that I grieve at the sight of the dangers which seem to threaten us, and I most heartily pray— " May this bitter cup be put far from us!" Not because they take our cloak, and can take our coat also; but because I dread a rupture, and the multitude of evils which may follow, although Religion can never perish!

If the Holy Father, whose heart is purity itself, would only represent to himself the benevolent acts of the French Monarchs

to

---

* A thousand shall fall at your right, and ten thousand at your left; and no evil shall approach you.

to the Holy See, he would not hesitate to comply with the desires of Louis XV. touching the Dutchy of Parma; but you know that every thing has two faces, and that the aspect under which some people present this affair to our Holy Father, is absolutely contrary to the views of the Sovereigns.

He will find the necessity of retreating; at least, if the present Pope does not, his successor must; which will be the more unlucky, as Clement XIII. is a Pontiff endowed with piety worthy of the first Ages of the Church, and deserves to be blessed by all the kingdoms who acknowledge his authority.

The Sacred College might remonstrate to him; but beside its being divided in sentiments about the affairs of Parma and the Jesuits, the Pope will do nothing which is not advised by his Council.

I do not at all wonder that Cardinal *** should so warmly interest himself for the Society and its General; there are very natural reasons for his attachment; but I am surprised at his being consulted in preference, considering that his sentiments upon

the

the subject are already universally known. In critical circumstances only, the opinions of those who are totally disinterested ought to be taken; otherwise, without intending, or even suspecting it, we become partizans of a faction.

It is our greatest glory to love only Truth, and to know her such as she is; so many illusions assume her appearance, that we are often deceived. When an occasion presents itself where we would see her without a cloud, we should divest ourselves of all we already know, and seek information as if we were totally ignorant of the matter; taking the advice of those who see and judge without prepossession.

Besides this, we ought to have a rectitude of intention, by which we may deserve to obtain supernatural lights; for the Lord trieth our hearts and reins; and if we are not animated with a love of justice in our researches, he abandons us to our own blindness.

I am, in all the fulness of my heart, &c.

Rome, 7th January, 1769.

LETTER CXXV.

TO A MONK OF HIS OWN ORDER.

PROVIDENCE, in raising me to the Cardinalship, has not made me forget my original lowliness; it is a view which is always present to me, and I find it an excellent preservative against every emotion of vanity. The dignity which I possess, and to which I was not born, has more thorns than roses, and in that resembles all eminent stations.

I am often obliged to be of a contrary opinion to the person in the world whom I respect most, and who deserves all my gratitude. It is the most cruel combat that my heart can sustain.

Charity, the inseparable companion of Truth, does not always speak the most pleasing language; but many people are deceived upon this subject, imagining that it ought to be always gentle, and always complying—in that case it would resemble flattery. There are circumstances where charity flames, lightens, and thunders. The Fathers of the Church who were filled with this spirit, when they spoke with the most anxious zeal, spoke with the voice of charity.

When you write to the Bishop of ***, make my most sincere compliments to him, and tell him, that every method has been employed to bring about an accommodation; but to no purpose. God (for we ought never to lose sight of him) will sooner or later make manifest his will.

You restore me to life, by telling me that our common friend is likely to recover. His understanding is of great use to those who consult him. He has an excellent talent for guiding the consciences of his penitents, without having the littleness of the major part of Directors; for it must be owned, that many men, who direct, have need themselves of being directed, as they are almost always ruined by women, who pay them a reverence due only to their God.---They look up to their spiritual guide, as if he was at least the Archangel Gabriel. It is undoubtedly right that they should have an esteem for those they consult,

sult, and whom they hear as the oracle of the Law; but that esteem should not be carried to excess.

They, who have a continual enthusiasm for their Directors, may be persuaded that some motives of mere human nature have mixed themselves up with such an attachment.

What a surprise will it be for a number of Devotées (who, believing themselves sincerely devoted to God, are only the worshippers of their Directors) when at the moment of their death they shall hear that dreadful sentence pronounced from the Supreme Mouth, "As I have not been the "object of your love, *depart, I know you not:*" *Discedite, nescio vos.*

This is what I have long shuddered at, on the articles of Directors. I could have wished that he who was formerly mine at Rome, and who died in the odour of sanctity, had made his manner of Directing, public. He was a man endowed with a large portion of the celestial spirit, who raised us above humanity, and wished to make us absolutely forget himself, and every object which did not attach us to God alone.

We want a good book upon the subject of Direction in Italy. We have a multitude, but they are only filled with common-place. To compose such a work, it is necessary, in the first place, to have the spirit of God; and secondly, an extensive knowledge of the human heart; for it is incredible with what address vanity and a thousand affections of the senses insinuate themselves at a time when we are persuaded that our sentiments are sublime, and worthy the attention of the Eternal. Hence springs the great difficulty in judging of ourselves.

I wish you every thing that you can desire, because I know that you desire nothing but what is highly commendable; and I am your dearest and most affectionate servant,

THE CARD. GANGANELLI.

CONVENT of the HOLY APOSTLES.

LETTER XXVI.

TO COUNT DE ***.

WE are at laſt ſummoned to a Conſiſtory, which is to determine affairs of the greateſt importance. We are to deliberate upon theſe unfortunate buſineſſes that have embroiled us for a conſiderable time with the Catholick Powers. Probably, the Holy Father, finding at laſt that he is not in a ſituation to reſiſt, will acquieſce in the requiſitions of the Houſe of Bourbon. He will at leaſt lay the reaſons of his diſſent before us for our conſideration, and every one will give his opinion.

I wiſh to God they had followed that plan from the beginning! But we do not often ſee the conſequences of a troubleſome affair till we are engaged in it.

I adviſe you to confer with ———; Rome, though renowned for politics, is not always ——— You underſtand me.

The Miniſters continue to make the moſt bitter complaints; and the intereſted parties,

parties, in order to prevent things from being brought to a conclufion, form circumvallations, blockades, and——Your own fenfe will tell you the reft.

There is every reafon for prefuming that France, Spain, and Portugal will, &c.

I will tell you nothing, if filence is impofed upon me, and certainly you will approve my conduct. I will not, like the little man in queftion, expofe myfelf to reproaches for having betrayed fecrets.

Befide the probity of a Cardinal, I have that natural rectitude which makes the effence of an honeft man, and which is a double engagement to be difcreet: but all of us will not be fufficiently fo, for I fufpect the affair will be inftantly divulged; and I fhall not be furprifed if the writers of the Dutch Gazettes fhould be informed of the whole.

I can know nothing before-hand, becaufe nothing tranfpires. The life which I lead here is of as dark a complexion as my habit, and confequently I am not to be found in thofe brilliant circles where great news is the subject of conversation. I only learn things by the means of our dear Abbé ———. But does he know every thing, and always speak truth? It is not because he means to deceive, but his imagination, his vivacity, &c.

I have again seen the Flying Post——— He has brought me the letters I expected; —they contain nothing but wise reflexions upon what I wanted to know. Adieu without ceremony, as you desired.

Rome, 31st January, 1769.

LETTER CXXVII.

TO THE SAME.

HERE is quite another affair on our hands than the Consistory I mentioned to you last post. The Holy Father, on going to-bed last night, was seised with a violent convulsion, uttered a great cry, and expired. We were to have met as this day, and to have drawn from the alembeck that which keeps all the Catholick Courts in suspence,

suspence, and has occasioned our being upon bad terms with them. Every one will reason differently upon this death, which has happened so extraordinarily in the present circumstances.

The excellent qualities of the late Pope, and the gratitude I owe to him, make me sincerely lament his death. Religion ought to compose his eulogy, and bewail the loss. He made himself truely respectable to all who approached him, by his most pleasing manners, which were pure as his intentions, and by a most incorruptible zeal: but I shall always say, that it was a pity he did not view things in their proper light.

He has left some Nephews deserving of the highest commendation for their excellent qualities, especially the Cardinal, who is one of the best men in the world.

The great difficulty now is, to know who will be chosen. I pity him before-hand, and I do not think it is right for me to say to you that it will be Such or Such-a one; for it is often the person who has been least thought of. One thing is certain, that I will not give my voice to any, but one in whom knowledge is joined with piety. A Pope, as Vicar of Jefus Chrift, ought to be infpired with true devotion; and as a temporal Prince to be poffeffed of a large fund of knowledge and fagacity. Happily, the Sacred College has many among its Members whom we may choofe with propriety. Pray that the Lord may infpire us, and give us a Chief according to his own heart, and the hearts of the Kings.

I have lately feen M. Morefofchi: he is a Prelate that deferves to be efteemed for his knowledge and candour.

The Conclave will be now more tolerable than in fummer. It will make no great change in my way of life. It is only quitting one cell to go into another: and if intrigues are formed, I proteft to you I fhall know nothing of them, being the man in the world who meddles the leaft in party matters.

You know my heart, and I need not fay to you that I am, &c.

Rome, 3d February, 1769.

LETTER CXXVIII.

TO A MONK, ONE OF HIS FRIENDS.

I AM going to the Conclave. Pray to God that he may bless our intentions, and restore to us a calm, after so long a storm.

I have been pressed to take a French Conclavist*. Besides that I have a predeliction for his nation, he has some excellent qualities; however, I will depend upon myself, that I may have nothing to fear from his indiscretion, if I should accept him, and he should be inclined to blab: *Secretum meum mihi*; *My secret is my own.*

Tell our Prelate that I could not answer his letter, but that I expect to see him at the Convent of the Holy Apostles, the day the Conclave breaks up. Minds are divided, but God can do what seemeth to him good, and it is his work that we are to be employed in.

* A Cardinal's Secretary while in Conclave.

Endeavour to procure for me the book I fpoke of, againſt the moment I recover my liberty. Adieu!

I am always your Friend and Servant.

Six in the morning.

LETTER CXXIX.

TO MONSIGNOR ***.

FOUR months are paſt, in which time I have not exiſted either to myſelf or my friends, but to all the different Churches, of which, by the Divine Permiſſion, I am become the Head; and to all the Catholick Courts, ſeveral of which, as you know, have very important affairs to regulate with the Court of Rome.

It was impoſſible to become Pope in more litigious times, and Providence has permitted the oppreſſive load to fall upon me. I hope that the Divine Grace will ſupport me, and give me the ſtrength and prudence which are indiſpenſably neceſſary to govern according to the rules of justice and equity.

I endeavour to take the most exact cognizance of the affairs which my Predecessor left me, and which cannot be finished but after a long examination.

You will do me a very great favour, if you will bring me what you have written upon the things which relate to this subject, and trust them to myself alone.

You will find me, as you have always known me, as much a stranger to the grandeur with which I am surrounded, as if I knew not even the name; and you may speak to me with the same frankness you used to do formerly, because the Popedom has given me a new love for truth, and a new conviction of my own nothingness.

Rome, 24th September.

LETTER CXXX.

TO A PORTUGUESE LORD.

YOU need not doubt of my having all possible desire to unite, more closely than ever, those ties which were lately between the Courts of Rome and Portugal attempted to be broken. I know how intimate a connection has always subsisted between these two Powers, from the earliest times, and shall be happy to place things on their old footing; but, as Common Father of the Faithful, and as Chief of all the Religious Orders, I shall do nothing until I have examined, weighed, and judged, according to the laws of justice and truth.

May God forbid that any human consideration should influence my decision! I have already a sufficiently severe account to render to God, without charging my conscience with the addition of a new crime; and it would be an enormous one, to proscribe a Religious Order, upon ru-
mours

mours and prejudices, or even upon fuspicions. I shall not forget, that *in rendering to Cæsar the things that are Cæsar's,* I ought to *render to God the things that are God's.*

I have already ordered a person to examine the Archives of the *Propaganda,* and to procure for me the correspondence of my illustrious brother and predecessor Sixtus Quintus with Philip II. Besides, I have required the heads of the accusation to be sent me, supported by such testimonies as cannot be rejected. I shall secretly become the Advocate of those whose ruin is demanded of me, that I may seek every means of justifying them within myself, before I pronounce.

The King of Portugal, as well as the Kings of France, Spain, and Naples, are too religious to disapprove of my proceeding.

If Religion requires sacrifices, all the Church shall hear me, and——

I wish it had been the will of Providence that I had not been reserved for such calamitous times; for in whatever way I act, I shall make some malecontents, I shall occasion murmurs, and render myself odious to a number of people whose esteem and friendship I sincerely desire.

I compare myself to one of the Prophets whom God raised in the midst of tempests; or to a soldier, who by his rank is exposed to combat, and though his views may be only to peace, yet by the post he holds, finds himself obliged to act, whether he likes it or not.

All is in the hands of God; may he direct my pen, my tongue, and my heart! I will submit to every thing, and I will do every thing that ought to be done, without dreading the consequences, &c.

LETTER CXXXI.

TO A MONK, ONE OF HIS FRIENDS.

IF you believe that I am happy, you are deceived. After having been agitated the whole day, I frequently wake in the middle of the night, and sigh for my Cloister,

Cloifter, my Cell, and my books. I may even fay, that I look upon your fituation with envy. What encourages me is, that God himfelf has placed me in the Chair of St. Peter, to the great furprife of the whole world; and if I am deftined to any important work, he will fupport me.

God knows, I would give every drop of my blood to have all pacified, that the whole world might return to their duty; that they who have given offenfe would reform, and that there might be neither divifion nor fuppreffion.

I will not come to the laft extremities, unlefs I am impelled by powerful motives; fo that pofterity at leaft may do me juftice, in cafe the prefent age refufe it to me. It is not that, however, about which I am anxious, but the Eternity to which I am fo near approaching, and which is a more formidable profpect to Popes than to any of the reft of the world.

I fhall fend you an anfwer to what you require. You know that I do not forget my friends, and that if I do not fee them so frequently as formerly, it is because business and sollicitude stand centries over me; they are at my gate, in my chamber, and in my heart.

Mention me to my old acquaintance: I think sometimes of the astonishment they must have been in at hearing of my elevation.

But more particularly tell him with whom I studied, that he did not prophesy well, when he told our companions that I should certainly end my days in France. There is no appearance of that being ever realised, or I must be destined for something very extraordinary indeed.

I am always your affectionate

CLEMENT.

At Castle Gandolpho.

LETTER CXXXII.

TO R. P. AIME DE LAMBALLE, GENERAL OF THE CAPUCHINS.

I AM sincerely obliged to you for the Prayers which you put up to Heaven for my preservation. I have doubly need
of

of them, as an individual, and as Head of the Church. I fhare all your pains and troubles, being convinced that you fuffer with a fpirit of penitence, and in a manner agreeable to God.

If you remain long at Paris, as I am afraid you muft on account of your indifpofition, you will have an opportunity of feeing M. Doria, whom I love in the fulnefs of my heart, as a Prelate who will one day be the joy and honour of the Church. I fee you in the midft of a world where there are great vices and great virtues; and where, by a particular Providence, the zeal for Religion, fo eminent in his Moft Chriftian Majefty, and all the Royal Family, and the great piety of the Prelate who holds the See of Paris, bids fair to ftop the progrefs of infidelity.

Bring with you fome French Monk, whofe knowledge will do honour to his nation in this country.

The Dominicans thought prudently when they called to the Minerva your worthy Countryman T. Fabrici, who will

perpetuate

perpetuate the glory of the Order by his learning.

If your illnefs does not prevent you from going to fee Madame Louife, I beg you will tell her how much I admire the facrifice fhe has made. Affure all your Brotherhood that I love them fincerely in the Lord, and that I exhort them to live always in a manner worthy of our Founder.

I fhall fpeak to Cardinal de Bernis upon what you defired me. You will have frequent enquiries made about him in France, for I know that he is as dear to the French as he is to the Italians.

I wifh to fee you again in good health, for I am entirely your's as before.

    (Signed) CLEMENT XIV.
ROME, 2d April, 1773.

BULL

BULL,
BRIEFS,
DISCOURSES, &c.
OF
CLEMENT XIV.

CIRCULAR LETTER

OF

CLEMENT XIV.

TO ALL

THE PATRIARCHS, PRIMATES, ARCH-BISHOPS AND BISHOPS

ON THE SUBJECT OF HIS ADVANCEMENT.

CLEMENT XIV.

TO OUR VENERABLE BRETHREN, HEALTH AND APOSTOLICAL BENEDICTION!

WHEN we consider the duties of the supreme Apostleship with which we have been clothed, we sink under so weighty a charge, and compare our situation to that of a man, who, drawn from the repose of a calm retirement, is cast into a tempestuous ocean, where he is on the point of being swallowed up by the waves. *But it is the work of the Lord, and it is wonderful in our eyes.* The inscrutable decrees of God, and not the counsels of men, have loaded us with the aweful duties of the

the Apostleship, when we were very far from entertaining any such thoughts. This conviction gives us a full confidence, that He who hath called us to the painful cares of the supreme Ministry, will condescend to calm our fears, assist our weakness, and hear our prayers. Peter, who ought to be our model, was encouraged by the Lord, and rebuked for his want of faith when he thought he was sinking in the sea. There is no doubt but that it is the will of our Divine Chief, who in the person of the Prince of Apostles, hath trusted to us the keys of the kingdom of Heaven, and hath commanded us to feed his sheep, that we put away all doubt of obtaining his aid. We submit ourselves then, without reserve, to Him, who is our strength and our help, resigning ourselves up to his power and truth. By his goodness he will complete in us the work which he hath begun; and even our lowness will serve to make his mercy shine forth with more lustre in the eyes of men: for if, in these wretched times, he hath resolved to accomplish something for the good of his Church by the ministry of so useless a servant as me, all mankind will evidently see that he is the Author and Perfecter, and that to him alone the glory ought to be ascribed. But the more powerful the help is upon which we depend, the more ought we to employ our efforts to co-operate with it; and the more exalted the honour to which we have been advanced, the more ought we to endeavour worthily to discharge its duties.

On whatever quarter of the Christian world we cast our eyes, we perceive you, our venerable Brethren, sharing with us in our glorious work; and this view fills us with consolation. It is with the greatest joy that in you we recognise our worthy assistants, faithful Pastors, and evangelical labourers. It is therefore that we are anxious to address ourselves to you at the beginning of our Apostleship. It is into your bosoms that we would pour the most secret sentiments of our soul; and if it appears that we offer you some exhortations, and give you some advice, attribute them solely to our distrust of ourselves, and think them the effects of that confidence which your virtues and filial love towards us have inspired.

First

First, we pray and befeech you, our venerable Brethren, to pray conftantly to God to ftrengthen our weaknefs: render us back this return of the tendernefs we bear towards you. Pray for our wants, as we pray for your's; fo that being mutually fuftained, we may be more firm and more vigilant. Let us prove by the union of our hearts, that unity by which we all make only one and the fame body; for the whole Church is but one building, of which the Prince of Apoftles laid the foundation here. Many ftones have been bound together for its conftruction; but all reft upon one alone, even upon Jefus Chrift, in whom we are all united as his members.

Being charged, as his Vicar, with the adminiftration of his power, we are raifed by his will to the moft eminent fituation; but united with us at the head of the vifible Church, you are the principal parts of that fame body. And as nothing can happen to us which will not affect you, fo there is nothing that can intereft you, but what muft become an object of our folicitude. It is therefore, that being in perfect

perfect agreement, and animated with the same spirit, which flowing from the Supreme Head, diffuses life through all the members, we ought chiefly to labour that the whole body of the Church be sound and intire, and neither contract spot or wrinkle, but flourish by the practice of every Christian virtue. With the Divine Help we may succeed in this, if every one, according to his power, would inflame himself with zeal in the care of the flock which is entrusted to him, and apply carefully to guard them from seduction, to procure them solid instructions, and the proper means of sanctification.

There never was a time when it was more necessary to watch for the safety of souls. Opinions most artfully calculated for shaking the cause of Religion are every day scattered abroad; and men in crouds allow themselves to be seduced by a thirst after novelty. It is a mortal poison, which insinuates itself into all conditions, and which makes the most cruel ravages.

My Reverend Brethren, it is a new motive for our labouring with more ardour than ever, to repress a madness which dares

to

to attack the most holy laws, and even to insult the Deity.

It is not by the help of human wisdom that you will succeed in this pious enterprise, but by the simplicity of the word of God, more piercing than a two-edged sword. You will easily repel all the attacks of the enemy; you will easily blunt all his arrows, by presenting in all your discourses only Jesus Christ, and Jesus Christ crucified. He hath built his Church, that Holy City, and furnished it with his Laws and his Precepts. He hath trusted to it the Faith which he came to establish, as a deposit to be religiously preserved in all its purity. It was his will that it should become the impregnable rampart of his Doctrine and Truth, and that the gates of Hell should never prevail against it. Being appointed to the care and government of this Holy City, our venerable Brethren, let us diligently preserve the Faith of our Holy Founder and Divine Master, that precious inheritance which our Fathers have transmitted to us, in all its purity, that we may transmit it equally pure to our descendents. If our actions

actions, and counsels are conformable to the rule marked out for us in the Holy Scriptures; if we walk in the paths of our Fathers, which cannot lead us astray; we may assure ourselves that we shall be able to shun every false step which is capable of weakening the Faith of the Christian people, or in any point injuring the unity of the Church. Let us only draw from the Scriptures, and from tradition, what it imports us to know and observe; these are the sacred sources of Divine Wisdom; and there we shall find whatever we ought to believe and practise; whatever concerns worship, discipline; or manner of living, is included in that double deposit. We shall there see the depth of our sublime Mysteries, the duties of Piety, the rules of Justice and Humanity. There we shall be instructed in what we owe to God, to the Church, to our country, and to our neighbour; and we must acknowledge that there is no law better than true Religion, to establish the rights of nations and society. The Doctrines of Jesus Christ have never been attacked without troubling the repose of the people, without disturb-
ing

ing the obedience due to Sovereigns, and without scattering troubles and confusion all around.

There is such an intimate union between the rights of his Divine Majesty, and the rights of the Kings of this world, that when the laws of Christianity are observed, Sovereigns are obeyed without regret, their power is respected, and their persons honoured.

We therefore exhort you, our venerable Brethren, to inculcate, to the utmost of your power, obedience and submission to Sovereigns in the people that are entrusted to your care; for among the Commandments of God, this is extremely necessary for preserving peace and good order. Kings have been elevated to the eminent ranks they possess, only to watch over the safety of the Publick, and to confine men within the bounds of wisdom and equity. They are the Ministers of God for the observance of justice, and they only carry the sword to execute the vengeance of God, by punishing those that stray from their duty. They are

are likewife the dear Children and the Protectors of the Church, and it is their duty to defend her rights, and fupport her interefts. Take care then, that you inftruct even the children, as foon as they are capable of it, to preferve an inviolable fidelity towards their Sovereigns, to fubmit to their authority, to obferve their laws, not only from the fear of punifhment, but as a duty enjoined by confcience.

When by your zeal and application you fhall have thus difpofed the minds of fubjects to obey their Kings, to refpect and love them in the fullnefs of their hearts, you will then have laboured effectually for the tranquillity of the people, and the good of the Church; for the one is infeparable from the other. But that you may infallibly acquit yourfelves with fuccefs in that duty, you fhould join to the Prayers which you daily make for the people, particular Prayers for the Kings, that you may obtain from God their prefervation and profperity, and the grace which is neceffary to govern with wifdom and with equity.

Thus, in labouring for the happiness of all mankind, you will worthily discharge the duties of your sacred Ministry; for it is just and right that the Pontiffs, who have been established for the good of man, in what concerns the worship of God, should present to God the vows of all the faithful, incessantly praying the Lord to support and establish him who watcheth for the publick tranquillity, and the preservation of all the people.

It would be superfluous to remind you of all the other obligations which the pastoral dignity imposes on you. You are already fully instructed in all the duties which the Christian Religion requires, living happily in the practice of all the virtues: for you should never fail to have Jesus Christ our Chief, the Prince of all Pastors, before your eyes, and still endeavour to render yourselves as near a copy as possible of that perfect model of Charity, Holiness, and Humility. Our labours, our thoughts, cannot have a more glorious or more excellent object than Him, who being the bright-

nefs

ness of his Father's glory, and the express image of his person, has been pleased to raise us to the quality of Children of God, by adoption, and to make us co-heirs with himself. It is the way to preserve the union and alliance of men with Jesus Christ, and to imitate that Divine Model of patience, gentleness, and humility. Wherefore it is said: *Ascend upon a high mountain, ye who preach the Gospel to Sion.*

If you have an ardent desire to conform to these duties, it is not possible but this holy ardour must by sympathy communicate itself from your heart to the breasts of all nations, and they become deeply inflamed with it; for the example of the Pastor has an astonishing virtue and power in moving the souls of the Faithful intrusted to his charge. When they perceive that all his thoughts and all his actions are regulated by the model of true virtue; when they see him avoid every thing which can relish of austerity, fierceness, and haughtiness; and employ himself only in works which inspire charity, gentleness, and humility;

humility; then they will find themselves animated to follow such an admirable and edifying example.

When they are convinced that a Pastor neglects himself to be useful to others; that his principal delight is to relieve the indigent; that he comforts the afflicted, instructs the ignorant, assists with his good offices and his counsels all those who stand in need of them; and, in a word, that every thing bespeaks a perfect disposition in him to sacrifice his life for the salvation of his people; then each individual struck with his virtues, and affected by his example, will enter into himself, and correct his faults. But if a Pastor, attached solely to his own interest, prefers the things of this world to those of Heaven, how can he engage his flock to love God only, and to render services to each other? If he sighs after riches, pleasures, and honours, how can he inspire the contempt of them? If he is haughty, and inflated with pride, how will he persuade them to be gentle and humble?

Since

Since then you are charged, our venerable Brethren, to form the people according to the maxims of Jesus Christ, your first duty is to live in the holiness, gentleness, and innocence of manners, of which he hath set us an example. You may depend upon it, you cannot make a proper use of your authority, but by endeavouring rather to give proofs of your modesty and charity, than by displaying the badges of your dignity. Be assured, that if you acquit yourselves scrupulously of the duties imposed upon you, you will be crowned with glory and happiness; and that, on the contrary, if you neglect them, you will be covered with shame, and prepare for yourselves the greatest of all miseries. Do not desire other riches than to secure those souls to God, which he hath purchased with his blood:—seek no other glory than that of consecrating yourselves entirely to the Lord, to labour incessantly in extending his worship, to set off the beauty of his House, to extirpate vice, and cultivate virtue. Such should be the sole object of

your

your thoughts, your defires, your actions, and your ambition. And do not think, our venerable Brethren, that after having paffed a long time in thefe painful labours, there will remain nothing more to exercife your virtue. Such is the nature of our Miniftry, fuch is the condition of a Bifhop, that he ought never to fee an end to his follicitude and cares; he can never give himfelf up to reft; for they whofe charity fhould know no bounds, ought to admit no bounds to their activity. The expectation of an eternal reward, is furely capable of rendering all our labour light.

Ah! what can appear difficult to men who keep conftantly in view the ineffable happinefs which the Lord will fhare with all thofe who faithfully watch and increafe his flock, when he comes to afk an account of their adminiftration! Befide this hope, fo fweet and precious, you will find inexpreffible joy and confolation in the very labours of an Epifcopal life. When God Almighty feconds our efforts, we fee the people ftrictly united by the ties of reciprocal

procal charity, and diftinguifhing themfelves by their innocence, candour, and piety: we fee a multitude of excellent fruits produced in the fields of the Church, by our watchings, fatigue, and cares.

May we, our moft dear and venerable Brethren, by our unanimous and voluntary agreement, zeal, and application, revive in the time of our Apoftlefhip that flourifhing ftate of Religion, and reftore all the beauty it poffeffed in the firft ages! May we be able to congratulate, and rejoice with, you in the Lord! May the God of mercy deign to fupport us by the help of his grace, and fill our hearts with whatever is agreeable to him!

In teftimony of our charity, We give you, with all poffible affection, and all the Faithful of your Churches, the Apoftolical Benediction.

At ROME, St. MARY MAJOR, the 12th of December, in the Year 1769, and the Firft of our Pontificate.

LETTER
TO HIS MOST CHRISTIAN MAJESTY, LOUIS XV.
UPON IRRELIGION.

WE know nothing more proper to kindle your zeal, than the motive which engages us to write to you. We do not purpose to speak at present of our personal interests, but those of Religion itself. If we are assured of your royal protection for ourselves, we have much more reason to believe that you will not reject our present sollicitations, which have no other view than the good of the Church.

It is the common cause of God and Christianity, which we at present plead before you, our most dear Son in Jesus Christ. We see with the deepest sorrow, the worship established by the Supreme Legislator, for a long time attacked by wicked men, who, without ceasing, direct against it the sacrilegious arrows of their perverse spirits. It may be said, that there is a general conspiracy, by the most audacious efforts, utterly to overthrow whatever is most venerable

able or sacred. They do not blush to produce every day a crowd of writings, an everlasting monument of their folly, in order to destroy even the first principles of good morals, to break the bonds of all Society, and to seduce simple souls, by the fatal talent which they possess of successfully sowing these perverse doctrines.

The astonishing rapidity of their progress persuades us, that there can be nothing more important, or more urgent, than to raise a mound to oppose this torrent.

It is not sufficient to take all the poisoned works which issue from that horrid School, out of the hands of the people; the zeal of our venerable Brethren the Bishops must come to our assistance; that by uniting our strength, we may, with one common accord, combat the different enemies of our Religion, and be avenged of the insults daily offered to it.

We see with inexpressible joy, upon this occasion, that the Prelates of Your Majesty's great and flourishing Empire, at present assembled in Paris for Ecclesiastical affairs, enter perfectly into our views,

views, and that their paftoral follicitude engages them to employ every means of ftopping the ravages of infidelity. We have a perfect confidence that in labouring, as they will do, in the caufe of God, they will receive abundantly the fpirit of wifdom and ftrength. It is no fmall confolation to us, to fee them apply with fo much zeal to the difcharge of fuch important duties.

But if they have need of the protection of the moft High, they have likewife a right to expect from you, our moft dear Son, the neceffary helps to affift and crown their labours. We therefore pray you, as much as in us lies, to favour them in whatever they do for the caufe of Religion, and to fupport them with vigour. Then will they give effectual proofs of the zeal which animates them, not only for the falvation of the Faithful, but for the temporal advantage of their Country, and alfo for your facred Perfon; for Religion being the firmeft fupport of Thrones, it is eafy to retain people who obey God, in obedience to Kings.

Hence

Hence it is eafy to be feen, that our cares and follicitude do not tend lefs to confirm your royal authority, than to maintain the interefts of God. Human focieties are much more indebted for their prefervation and fecurity to the exercife of the true worfhip, and the ftability of the revealed doctrine, than to the force of arms, or the abundance of riches.

The true way of drawing down the moft precious effects of the Divine mercy upon your facred Perfon, and upon the Princes and Princeffes of your blood, is publickly to maintain the Faith and Piety in their purity. By doing this you will fhow yourfelf eminently fkilled in the art of reigning, that art by which your anceftors have always fhown themfelves Moft Chriftian Kings; and you will fupport your own glory and their's, by adding the moft ftriking proofs of your Religion to their example.

This fubject would no doubt require to be treated more fully; but the high opinion we have of your truely royal Piety, makes us look upon a long Difcourfe on this fubject as fuperfluous.

In the firm perfuafion that Your Majefty will grant what we afk with equal zeal and juftice, we pray the Almighty, by whom you reign, that he may long preferve you and your Auguft Family; and we give you, with all poffible tendernefs, our Apoftolical Benediction. May it be a happy prefage of the favour and happinefs which we wifh you!

ROME, 21ft March, 1770.

TO MADAME LOUISE OF FRANCE, CLEMENT XIV.

TO OUR MOST DEAR DAUGHTER IN JESUS CHRIST, ALL HEALTH!

IT feemeth to us that the moft painful labours of the Apoftlefhip with which we have been clothed, are become light and pleafing, fince we have learnt your holy and generous refolution. You could undertake nothing more grand nor more fublime than to exchange the pomp of a Royal Court for the humiliation of a Religious Houfe.

Whether

Whether we confider the pious condefcenfion of our moft dear Son in Jefus Chrift, Louis, your Auguft Father, and Moft Chriftian King, who has permitted you to make fuch a facrifice; or look upon the precious advantage which muft thence refult to the Church; we cannot contain our joy and admiration.

May thanks be rendered to God, the Authour of all good, that he has given us, in your perfon, fuch a ftriking example to all Princes, and all Nations, and has deigned to confecrate our Pontificate by fo glorious an event. It is a fubject of congratulation for us, as well as for you. Ah! how can we be otherwife than delighted with the view of the abundant riches which the Lord hath heaped upon you; and with that all-divine ftrength which made you, after the moft mature reflections, embrace a kind of life which may be called a fketch of Heaven! None but God himfelf could infpire you with fuch a generous defign. You have learnt, by the favour of Divine illumination, that all the grandeurs of this world are only vapours; all its pleafures, mere illusions; all its promises, arrant falsehoods; and lastly, that the soul can only find peace in the pleasing exercise of the love of God; and that you cannot reign, but by serving him alone.

Now it is, that, in the port where you are at present, sheltered from rocks and shipwreck, you are about to enjoy the most delicious tranquillity; to taste, more than ever, the holy and divine pleasures which are the inheritance of the friends of God. When we can triumph over the world, we possess the greatest riches, in the midst of indigence. We find true liberty in renouncing ourselves; grandeur and glory in the depressions of the profoundest humility. Nothing is comparable to the happiness of concentrating all our thoughts, and all our desires, in the bosom of God; to live with Him alone, to be inflamed with the love of Him, and to have no other hope but that of possessing Him for ever.

May your courage increase, our most dear Daughter, in proportion as the grace of God has been plentifully poured upon you! Persevere, with all your strength, in the noble defign which you have formed, of proceeding in the way of Salvation. Make that Being the conftant object of your thoughts, whom you have propofed to love and ferve all the days of your life; think that the recompence which is the object of your defires, is infinite; and the fruit which you expect, incorruptible: By that means you will change your labours into delights, and you will tafte before-hand the fweets of a Heaven to come.

The more we reflect upon the generous ftep which you have taken, the more we rejoice in the hope, that the brilliant example will produce in many other people the defire of imitating it. You will not fail to call to mind that the King, your indulgent Father, having facrificed the pleafure he had in your fociety, that he might not oppofe your call, you ought to employ every means of teftifying your gratitude towards him. The only way to acquit yourfelf is, to pray continually to God, to make him happy in this life, and in that which is to come.

Your

Your zeal for the Church, which is well known to us, together with your refpectful attachment to the Holy See, are new motives of joy and confolation; for we are perfuaded that you will apply conftantly to God for our particular wants, as well as thofe of Religion. We offer you, in acknowledgement of all thefe good offices, every advantage which you can expect from our paternal tendernefs. Nothing can equal the extreme defire which we have to fecond your pious intentions, and to promote the fervour with which you walk in the paths of virtue. And although we are perfectly convinced of your zeal and perfeverance, we will willingly give to your prefent or future Confeffor the power of foftening your Rule, and even of difpenfing with it in every cafe where your weaknefs cannot keep pace with your courage. Befides, we grant you, in virtue of our Apoftolical authority, a full and entire indulgence every time you approach the Holy Table; and to teftify our affection ftill more, we grant the fame favour to our Holy Daughters in Jefus Chrift

Chrift, your worthy Companions, and make them participators with you in our Apoftolical Benediction.

Given at ROME, 9th May, 1770, the firft Year of our Pontificate.

LETTER
TO HIS MOST CHRISTIAN MAJESTY, LOUIS XV.

ON THE SUBJECT OF MADAME LOUISE TAKING THE HABIT.

OUR MOST DEAR SON IN JESUS CHRIST, ALL HEALTH!

IT is proper, that at the fame time we write to our moft dear Daughter in Jefus Chrift, the Princefs Louifa Maria, to congratulate her on the greatnefs of her facrifice, we pour forth our joy into the paternal bofom of your Majefty. You have given us the greateft delight; and the more fo, as you have had the principal fhare in fo remarkable and fo fplendid an action. But what fills our Soul with infinite fatisfaction, is, that after having applauded

plauded the generous proceeding of your August Daughter, you have shown extraordinary courage, in separating yourself from her, notwithstanding the inestimable qualities which rendered her so dear to you; and that as soon as you believed you heard the voice of Religion, you stifled the call of Nature, and have only seen a future Spouse for Jesus Christ, in her who was your beloved Daughter. Thus you yourself have opened the way to Heaven to a pious Princess who desired with ardour to enter it; and you have contributed, by your generous approbation, to secure her from the dangers which surround human life, and the tumultuous waves which distract it.

I see her in the holy retreat which she hath chosen, teaching the whole world that there is nothing more frail, nor more vain, than all the delights and all the grandeur of this life: that they are to be looked upon only as rocks, which often become the lamentable cause of a multitude of evils, by opposing the acquisition of eternal happiness.

The

The share which you have had in so pious an action, ought to give you the greatest confidence in the prayers of your illustrious Daughter: she will never cease to pray to God for your August Person, your Royal Family, and your whole Kingdom, and, what should still more interest your Majesty, for the salvation of your soul. It is a powerful intercession which you have obtained in the sight of the Almighty; and it much concerns you to derive every possible advantage from an event which Providence has permitted for your good.

We wish, in the fullness of our heart, that you would receive the testimonies of our affection, as the tender overflowings of the heart of a Father who dearly loves you, and who is no less zealous for your glory and happiness than his own. To convince you of it, we give you, our most dear Son in Jesus Christ, in the most affectionate manner possible, our Apostolical Benediction, as an undoubted proof of the singular love that, &c.

Given at ROME, 9th May, 1770, and the First of our Pontificate.

A SECOND LETTER

TO HIS MOST CHRISTIAN MAJESTY, LOUIS XV.

ON THE SAME SUBJECT

AFTER having congratulated Your Majesty, by our Letter of the 9th of May laſt, on the heroic courage with which the Princeſs Louiſa, your Auguſt Daughter, is about to embrace a religious life; after having teſtified to her the fullneſs of our joy on the ſame ſubject; we cannot reſiſt again expreſſing our ſatisfaction, and tranſports we feel at the approach of ſuch a ſacrifice. Her zeal is ſo ardent, that ſhe can ſuffer no longer delay, and ſhe is inflamed with the deſire of ſeeing herſelf clothed in the holy Habit of the Carmelites, by the hands of our Venerable Brother, Bernardin, Archbiſhop of Damaſcus, our Nuncio in Ordinary to Your Majeſty.

From

From the firſt news we received of her generous deſign, we recogniſed the ſpirit of God acting in a moſt wonderful manner on the ſoul of this Auguſt Princeſs; and we found ourſelves affected with the ſtrongeſt deſire to go in perſon to perform the ceremony of the *Veſture*, which our Nuncio is to perform, and thereby augment the luſtre and ſolemnity of ſo great a day. But the diſtance making it impoſſible, we ſhall accompliſh our deſires in part, by charging our Nuncio, our Brother above-named, with this auguſt duty. We will ſeem to aſſiſt in ſome ſort ourſelves, and lead our moſt dear daughter in Jeſus Chriſt to the nuptials of her Divine Spouſe. We pray you to approve of the Letters which we have addreſſed on that ſubject to the Nuncio who repreſents us; and we perſuade ourſelves that you will acquieſce the more willingly, as theſe diſpoſitions have no other motive than our zeal and affection for your Majeſty.

As a certain pledge of theſe ſentiments, and as a happy preſage of the divine bleſſing, receive our Apoſtolical Benediction.

We

We give it with all the tenderness of a Father to you, and to all your August Children, especially the pious Princess who is the memorable subject of our gladness.

> Given at ROME, the 18th of July, 1770, the second Year of our Pontificate.

SECOND LETTER

TO MADAME LOUISE, OF FRANCE.

OUR MOST DEAR DAUGHTER IN JESUS CHRIST, ALL HEALTH!

AT last the most glorious and the most fortunate day of your life approaches; a day on which, by the most sacred and intimate ties, you are to become the Spouse of Jesus Christ himself; and devote to him all your desires, all your thoughts, and all your actions.

We were transported with joy, and we applauded your magnanimity, from that moment, when, treading the vanities of the world under your feet, you renounced the delights of the most brilliant Court, to confine

confine yourself to the obscurity of the Cloister, and there to make trial of the most humble and most mortifying life: but your publick profession, by which you are about to make Heaven and Earth witnesses of your generous sacrifice, completes your joy. Never forget that the Lord, by calling you from the bosom of Grandeur to live under the shadow of the Cross, marked you with the Seal of Predestination. The higher the rank you held in the world, the more is his goodness remarkable, and the more ought your soul to be penetrated with love and gratitude.

All the festivals of this world have nothing to compare with that great day, when, led by the inspiration of Grace, you shall give yourself up entirely to God, and solemnly take Him for your inheritance.

Would to Heaven, our dearest Daughter, that it were possible for us to assist in person at this august ceremony, to be not only a witness, but likewise the Minister of such an heroick sacrifice! Nevertheless, although that happiness is denied us, we we will not fail to enjoy it as much as poſſible, by having ourſelves repreſented by our venerable Brother, the Archbiſhop of Damaſcus, our Nuncio in ordinary. It was already by his hands that we clothed you in the ſacred habit, and it will be by him that we ſhall receive your ſacred vows; and that nothing may be wanting for the ſolemnity of ſo great a day, we charge him to impart to you all the treaſures of the Church.

We do not doubt of your ſhowing every ſenſe of our paternal tenderneſs, by advancing more and more in the courſe you have entered, and by the conſtant practice of all the virtues, more eſpecially that of humility. It is from thence you will learn that you ought not to be vain of any thing, but that you hold all from God; that you ought conſtantly to diſtruſt your own ſtrength, and not rely on your own merit, but on his Almighty Grace only; believing, at the ſame time, that you are capable of every thing in Him who ſtrengthens you, and never ceaſing to have recourſe to his infinite mercy.

Theſe

These sentiments, deeply engraved on your soul, will diffuse a Christian modesty over your whole behaviour; and in the shadow of that humility, Divine Love will take root in your heart, and will produce fruit both useful and abundant.

It is not by way of advice that we speak to you in this manner, as if we thought you had need of it, but to render the way of life to which God hath called you, more precious in your eyes.

You will certainly make it a capital duty to testify, upon all occasions, the lively gratitude which you owe to your August Father, who has loved you so tenderly, and done every thing for you: you will never cease to pray to God to preserve him, to prosper his kingdom and his august Family, and, above all, to grant him eternal happiness.

As for us, if we may be permitted to claim the rights which our affection entitles us to, we conjure you to draw down upon our person, as your Father in Jesus Christ, the favourable attention of the Lord, and to pray continually for the Church entrusted

trusted to our care. And now that you are more intimately attached to her, you ought to interest yourself more than ever in what concerns either her advantage or glory. On your part, you may be persuaded that we will continually beg of God to bless your pious resolutions, and that you may increase more and more in his holy love.

Receive, as a pledge of our paternal affection, our Apostolical Benediction; we give it with all our heart to you, and likewise to all the Order of Carmelites, with whom you are about to be associated for ever.

<blockquote>Given at ROME, at St. MARY-MAJOR, under the FISHERMAN's-RING, the 14th of August, 1771, and the third Year of our Pontificate.</blockquote>

LETTER

TO MONSIGNOR BERNARDIN GIRAULT, ARCH BISHOP OF DAMASCUS, NUNCIO TO HIS MOST CHRISTIAN MAJESTY.

TO OUR VENERABLE BROTHER, HEALTH AND APOSTOLICAL BENEDICTION!

IT has been reprefented to us, that the Princefs Louife-Marie of France, our moft dear Daughter in Jefus Chrift, retired to the Monaftery of the Bare-footed Carmelites of St. Denis, defires with the moft lively ardour to embrace their holy inftitution, and that in order more fully to fatisfy her devotion, fhe is to receive the habit at your hands, as being Superior of the Order.

When we think of that Princefs, born in the midft of the delights and grandeur of the moft brilliant Court in the world, devoting herfelf to the moft auftere and retired life, we cannot help admiring, and at the fame time acknowledging the impreffion of the Holy Ghoft, fo as to fay, 'It is a miracle of the Moft High.' We are fo

deeply

deeply penetrated on this occafion, that to accord with the inexpreffible fentiments of the zeal with which we are animated, and the joy which tranfports us, we charge you to perform this ceremony in our name.

Therefore, to give to this holy and celebrated Office all the luftre which it merits, and all the folemnity of which it is fufceptible, we fpecially depute and delegate you, our venerable Brother, to act for us in our place.

This interefts us the more deeply, as we fhall believe we are there prefent, to fee with our own eyes with what holy tranfports our moft dear Daughter in Jefus Chrift will unite herfelf, with all her heart, to her heavenly Hufband.

Befides this, as we are defirous to augment, and render more complete, the general fatisfaction of the Order, by giving to all thofe who compofe it the fpiritual treafures of the Church; WE, out of our free benevolence, grant plenary indulgence to all the Bare-footed Carmelites of the kingdom of France, who, on the day

the

the Princefs takes the habit, shall partake of the Sacraments of Penitence and the Eucharist, and implore the mercy of the Almighty for the exhaltation of the Holy Catholick Church, for our most dear Son in Jesus Christ Louis Most Christian King of France, for his Children, for the Royal Family, and particularly for the Princefs who is at present the subject of our joy, and who is to begin her Noviciate in the most austere and sacred state; that new grace may be heaped upon her from day to day; that she may become more the ornament of her Order by the regularity of her life, than by the splendour of her name.—And you, our venerable Brother, we desire you diligently to inform all whom it may concern, of the salutary favour with which we are willing to gratify them: and for a proof of our Pontifical good will, we give you, &c.

Rome, 18th July, 1770, the second Year of our Pontificate.

LETTER
TO HIS MOST CHRISTIAN MAJESTY,

OUR MOST DEAR SON IN JESUS CHRIST,
ALL HEALTH!

EVERY time we think of your illuſtrious Daughter, Louiſe-Marie of France, who in Jeſus Chriſt is likewiſe our's, we bleſs God that he hath ſo inſpired her. —We have conſtantly before our eyes the great example which ſhe ſets to the world; an example which will do honour to this age, and will be the admiration of poſterity. The nearer the moment of the ſacrifice approaches, the more we redouble our prayers, and the more we deſire to declare to you the ſentiments which attach us to your perſon, by rendering the tribute of praiſe which is due to you for the part you have taken in this great event, of which the Church is to be the witneſs.

Undoubtedly you could not do better than ſecure to yourſelf a ſupport in the prayers and vows of her who is totally devoted to

your

your perfon, and is entirely agreeable to God. In this your wifdom is as eminent as your Religion; and that perfuades us, at the fame time, that by the Divine goodnefs you will reap the greateft advantage from fo favourable an event. We congratulate you with all our heart, and applaud ourfelves, becaufe the union with our moft dear Daughter in Jefus Chrift will become more ftrong than ever. Our greateft defire would be to tie thefe knots ftill more clofely, by prefiding at the ceremony which we fee approaching, and receiving in perfon the moft folemn vows which the moft tender piety can pronounce.

We are the more penetrated with this thought, as it would be a moft happy occafion of converfing with you, of embracing you, and fhowing you in our eyes, and on our countenance, the fentiments with which you infpire us. Then our paternal tendernefs and our paftoral charity fhining forth, would affure you in the ftrongeft manner of our entire affection. But, alas! we are so unfortunately situated, as to have that satisfaction only in idea.

As to any other advantages, we have endeavoured to procure them, notwithstanding our absence; having chosen our venerable Brother the Archbishop of Damascus to supply our place, and given him the most special and extensive powers for that purpose, as we before did, when we gave him commission to represent us at the ceremony of taking the Habit.

Being informed that your Majesty then approved of the manner in which we regulated the ceremony of giving the Habit to our August Princess, we flatter ourselves that you will equally approve at present of the same dispositions.

We earnestly pray you, then, to join in our views, with your usual goodness, and afford us the consolation to see our place supplied by our Representative.

Receive, as the best proof which we can give of our attachment, our Apostolical Benediction, which, as a pledge of all the benedictions of Heaven, shall extend to your

your auguft race, and over your whole kingdom, if our prayers are heard.

Given at ROME, at St. MARIE-MAJOR, under the FISHERMAN's-RING, the 14th of Auguft, 1771, the third year of our Pontificate.

LETTER

TO THE DUKE OF PARMA.

IT would be very difficult to exprefs all the fatisfaction which your letter gave us, in which we find fentiments of the moft tender affection. We are the more happy at prefent to receive fuch marks of your friendfhip, as we have always been moft fingularly attached to you, and have never ceafed to intereft ourfelves in whatever could concern you.

We congratulate ourfelves, at the fame time, on your having received with all poffible good-will the teftimonies of our friendfhip (on account of the illuftrious offspring that will one day be the heir of your virtues) and the proof of our acknowledgements for the zeal with which you laboured

boured for our reconciliation with his Moſt Chriſtian Majeſty. By it you have completed the proofs of your piety towards the Holy See, and have taken a ſtep equally glorious and meritorious. The mediation which you have employed with our dear Sons in Jeſus Chriſt, the moſt virtuous Kings your Grandfather, Uncle, and Couſin, to engage them to erafe from their minds every trace of old miſunderſtandings, and to réſtore to us the domains of Avignon, Benevento, and Porto Corvo, cannot fail to be moſt effectual. You do us juſtice in being convinced of our extreme love for peace and concord, particularly with the auguſt Houſe of Bourbon, which has always deferved ſo well from us, from the Chair of St. Peter, and the whole Church in general.——We never doubted that the Religion and wiſdom of theſe Sovereigns would inſpire them with the ſame pacifick ſentiments which we cheriſh in our own breaſt. Your royal virtues and the affection which your auguſt relations moſt reaſonably bear to you, inſpire us with the ſtrongeſt hopes from your mediation. They will join with

with more zeal to fecond your good intentions, when they fee peace and harmony reftored from the fame fource from whence the mifunderftanding and difagreement proceeded. In return, we will feife every opportunity of proving to you, in the moft diftinguifhed manner, our gratitude and affection.

With all the tendernefs of paternal affection, we give our Apoftolical Benediction to you, as likewife to your virtuous Spoufe, and to your dear new-born Son; and we pray the Almighty God that you may increafe in virtue from day to day, and acquire that glory which he hath referved for the Elect.

SECOND LETTER

TO THE DUKE OF PARMA.

AS foon as we were informed of the pains you had taken to reconcile us with the Kings our moft dear Sons in Jefus Chrift, and reftore to the Holy See its ancient poffeffions, we refolved to render you our moft fincere thanks. Now that your wifdom has completed this great work, we muft publickly proclaim our joy and gratitude. We affure you that we will never forget this generous proceeding, which has procured us fuch fignal advantages; and that the paternal tendernefs which we have for you is equal to your great virtues. We therefore pray, in the fullnefs of our heart, for whatever can contribute to your glory and happinefs. The Marquis de Lano, to whom we are tenderly attached, on account of his merit and fervices to us, has doubtlefs declared to you what our fentiments are with regard to you. It is to confirm them more and more, that we
continually

continually pray to God to fecond, by the abundance of his heavenly gifts, the Apoftolical Benediction with which we falute you as the moft certain pledge of our affection, &c.

BRIEF.

TO OUR DEAR SON PETER FRANCIS BOUDIER, AT PRESENT SUPERIOR-GENERAL OF BENEDICTINES, OF THE CONGREGATION OF ST. MAUR, AND GRAND PRIOR OF THE ROYAL ABBEY OF ST. DENNIS.

CLEMENT XIV.

TO OUR DEAR SON, HEALTH AND APOSTOLICAL BENEDICTION!

YOUR Letter, dictated by refpect, attachment, and moft tender love, evidently proves the joy which you and your Congregation felt upon our elevation to the Sovereign Pontificate. Your fentiments for the Apoftolical Chair were already known to us, and the new teftimonies which you give us of them, were not wanted

wanted to perfuade us of your attachment to the Holy See.

We have likewife been very fenfible of the demonftrations of zeal, to which you and your congregation have added a new value, by praying the Father of Mercies to fupport and fortify our weaknefs, by his powerful help, in the adminiftration of fuch an important employment.

As to the judgment which you have formed of Us, We fee nothing but your indulgence, your filial love, and the ardent zeal with which you are animated for Us. On Our part, We exceedingly defire to have fome opportunity of teftifying all the good-will we bear towards you, and thofe who are fubmitted to your care. In the mean time, as a pledge of our paternal tendernefs, We give to you, Our dear Son, and to your Brethren, with the fulleft effufion of Our heart, Our Apoftolical Benediction.

Given at ROME, at St. MARIE-MAJOR, under the FISHERMAN's-RING, the 11th Auguft, 1769, and the Firft Year of our Pontificate.

BENEDICT STAY.

BRIEF

TO OUR DEAR SON BODDAERT, PRIOR-GENERAL OF THE ORDER OF GUILLELMITES.

CLEMENT XIV.

TO OUR DEAR SON, HEALTH AND APOSTOLICAL BENEDICTION!

THE joy which you teftify at Our advancement to the Sovereign Pontificate agrees with the attachment which your Order has a long time had for us. We do not doubt of your adding to thofe exterior proofs of your zeal, the affiftance of your prayers to God that he will deign to help our weaknefs; and therefore we at prefent requeft the continuance of them, as the effect of your charity for us. As to our fentiments with regard to you, the inftances which we have formerly given of our good-will towards you, fufficiently fhow what you may expect. Be affured that our new dignity, far from leffening that good-will, has rather increafed it; efpecially after the teftimony you have given us, that having carefully vifited the Monafteries of your Order, you have found them

them obedient to the Rules of their Inftitution. This affurance on your part has given us the greateft pleafure—it redoubles the tendernefs which we have for you; and to give you a pledge of it, we grant to you, our dear Son, and to all the Order intrufted to your care, with all the effufion of our heart, Our Apoftolical Benediction.

Given at ROME, at St. MARIE-MAJOR, under the FISHERMAN'S-RING, the 9th of July, 1769, and the Firft of our Pontificate.

BENEDICT STAY.

SPEECH OF CLEMENT XIV.
IN THE SECRET CONSISTORY HELD THE 21ft OF SEPTEMBER, 1770.

ON THE SUBJECT OF THE RECONCILIATION OF PORTUGAL WITH THE COURT OF ROME.

IT feems, our venerable Brethren, that Providence hath chofen this day, the twenty-fourth of the month, for me to notify to you the great event on account of which we are affembled in this place this day, which is the anniverfary of my arrival in Rome; of my advancement to the Purple, however unworthy of the honour; and

and I am to announce to you a full and entire reconciliation with the court of Portugal.

We have juſt received the moſt ſincere and the moſt eminent proofs of the ſubmiſſion and zeal of his Moſt Faithful Majeſty——they have even ſurpaſſed our expectation. The correſpondence and attachment which had ever before ſubſiſted between us and that Crown are not only again renewed, but likewiſe confirmed in ſuch a manner that they have acquired new ſtrength.

When we foretold what has juſt now happened, we founded our hopes upon the faith and piety of our moſt-dear Son in Jeſus Chriſt, who at all times has given the moſt unqueſtionable proofs of his zeal for the true Religion. The day we were informed of his reconciliation, increaſed the glory and advantage of the Holy See, by filling us with conſolation and joy. There is, therefore, nothing which we ought not to undertake to teſtify our acknowledgements to his Moſt Faithful Majeſty, and no wiſh which we ought not to form for his

his prefervation, and that of Marie-Anne-Victoire, his auguft and dear Spoufe, who rivalled him in her great zeal to bring about this accommodation. The Count d'Oyeras, Secretary of State, is equally deferving of our gratitude and praife; and we ought not to forget the Governor of Almada, Minifter Plenipotentiary with Us; whom we have often heard, with the greateft joy, declare to us the pious and laudable fentiments of his Moft Faithful Majefty. As there is no method more proper to acquit ourfelves of our gratitude to a Prince fo deferving of praife, than to pray God to profper him; let us beg of him continually to grant us that great favour, &c.

SPEECH

SPEECH OF CLEMENT XIV.

IN THE SECRET CONSISTORY, HELD THE 6th OF JUNE, 1774,

UPON THE DEATH OF LOUIS XV.

VENERABLE BRETHREN,

COULD any thing have confoled us in the midſt of our painful labours, it was our knowledge of the rectitude of intention and attachment to Religion, as well as to our own perſon, ſo eminent in Louis, the Moſt Chriſtian King; but, alas! that confolation becomes now the ſubject of the deepeſt ſorrow. Our life has been a ſtate of affliction ever ſince we heard of his death; an event truely fatal, and the conſequence of a moſt cruel diſorder. We are the more deeply affected, as we have loſt him in that moment, when he had given us the moſt conſpicuous proofs of his juſtice, magnanimity, and tender affection towards us and the Holy Apoſtolical See. And what afflicts us yet more, is, that

that we cannot now acquit ourselves towards him, but by our tears and our regret.

Neverthelefs, let us adore the decrees of Divine Providence; and in fubmitting to the will of the Almighty, upon whom the fate of Kings abfolutely depends, let us acknowledge that all is directed by his wifdom, and for his glory.

Nothing but this refignation to the Divine Will can leffen our forrow. We no. fooner heard the danger with which the King's life was threatened, than we addreffed our moft fervent prayers to Heaven, to obtain his recovery. All France united their fupplications with our's, and all the Royal Family, fhedding torrents of tears, acquitted themfelves of the fame duty; particularly our moft dear daughter in Jefus Chrift, Marie-Louife of France, who from her hóly retreat raifed her pious hands towards Heaven, and gave vent to the deepeft forrow.

If our vows have not been heard, we have at leaft a lively hope that our prayers

may

may be useful for the repose of his soul, and procure him eternal glory.

Our hope is founded upon the love which he always professed for the Catholick Religion; his attachment to the Holy See; his good intentions towards us, of which he gave us proofs to the last moment; and lastly, upon the sincere repentance which he testified in presence of his whole Court, begging pardon of God, and his kingdom, for the errors of his life, and desiring to live only to repair them

The same prayers which we have put up in secret for the repose of his soul, We shall put up also in publick: yet That shall not hinder us from remembering him before God, to the last hour of our life.

It is requisite upon this occasion to declare to you, our venerable Brethren, that Louis Augustus, our most dear Son in Jesus Christ, Grandson of the late King, succeeds to the Estates and Kingdoms of his Grandfather, inheriting, at the same time, all the heroick virtues of the August House of Bourbon.

We

We already know his zeal and attachment to Religion, as well as his filial love towards us. His pathetick letters filled with affection, joined to the fame of his excellent qualities, which are every where published, are the most convincing proofs how well we have founded our expectations. We have nothing more at heart than to answer, as much as we possibly can, such laudable sentiments.

We at the same time inform you, that our venerable Brother Francis-Joachim, Cardinal of Bernis, formerly Ambassador from the late King to our Person, hath been continued in the same character by his credentials, which he hath presented to us. In showing you our perfect satisfaction upon that subject, we observe your's to shine forth; knowing that you are persuaded, as well as we, that he is a most faithful interpreter both of the King's intentions and ours, in order to preserve a happy harmony.

Let us by our most ardent prayers conjure the Almighty, from whom Kings hold their crowns and kingdoms, to shed his most
abundant

abundant bleſſings upon our moſt dear Son in Jeſus Chriſt, Louis-Auguſtus of France, that in the courſe of his reign he may enjoy all proſperity, and live in ſuch a manner as to be uſeful to the cauſe of Religion, and advantageous to the illuſtrious French nation.

BULL

FOR THE

UNIVERSAL JUBILEE,

IN THE YEAR MDCCLXXV.

CLEMENT, Biſhop, Servant of the Servants of God, to all the Faithful in Jeſus Chriſt, to whom theſe Letters ſhall come, Health and Apoſtolical Benediction.

Jeſus Chriſt our Lord, the Author of our Salvation, not ſatisfied with procuring to man, by his death and paſſion, a deliverance from the old ſlavery of ſin, a return to life and liberty, an exaltation to
the

the sublime title of Co-heirs to his glory, and Children of God; has added to all these favours one infinitely precious, and destined for those, who, drawn aside by human frailty, and their own perverseness, have unfortunately forfeited the right they had to the Divine inheritance. By the power to remit sins, which he gave to the Prince of Apostles when he entrusted him with the keys of the kingdom of Heaven, he has procured to sinners a means of expiating their transgressions, of recovering their first innocence, and receiving the fruits of Redemption. As it is the only means they possess, who have deviated from the law of the Lord, to re-enter into friendship with God, and to attain eternal salvation, the successors of St. Peter, the heirs of his power, have never had any thing more at heart than to summon all sinners to the divine source of mercy, to offer and promise pardon to true penitents, and to invite even those who are held in heavy chains of sin to the hopes of remission.

Although

Although the exercise of a duty of this importance, so necessary for man's salvation, has never interrupted the cares of their Apostolical Ministry; they have nevertheless judged proper to choose and fix, in the course of ages, certain remarkable periods for engaging sinners to soften the Divine wrath, to embrace penitence as the only plank which remains after shipwreck; and that by the hope of a more ample harvest of graces and pardons, and by the public and general liberty to share the treasures of indulgence of which they are the depositaries.—And that no generation might be deprived of the precious advantages attached to these times of relaxation, they have fixed the return of every twenty-fifth year as the year of Jubilee, the holy year, the year of grace and remission, which they have ordered to be opened in the City which is looked upon as the center and seat of Religion.

We then, in conformity with so salutary a custom, and one of these privileged years being at hand, are anxious to announce it to all of you, our dear Children, who are

united

united in the profeſſion of the ſame faith with us, and the holy Roman Catholick Church; and we exhort you to labour for the good of your ſouls, and to profit by ſuch means of ſanctification as may be moſt effectual. We offer you a ſhare of all the riches of the Divine mercy and clemency which have been entruſted to us; and chiefly of thoſe which have their origin in the blood of Jeſus Chriſt. We will then open to you all the gates of the rich reſervoir of Atonement derived from the merits of the Holy Mother of God, the holy Apoſtles, the blood of the Martyrs, and the good works of all the Saints, ſo great and ſincere is our deſire to facilitate to you the recovery of peace and reconciliation.

Now, nothing contributes more than the multitude of helps which may be expected from the Communion of the Saints. United to their auguſt ſociety, we with them compoſe the body of the Church, which is one indiviſible, and that of Jeſus Chriſt himſelf, whoſe blood purifies us, enlivens us, and puts us in a condition to be uſeful to one another. For to give more luſtre to
the

the immensity of his love and mercy, to render more sensible the strength and infinite efficacy of his Passion and his merits, the Redeemer of mankind hath been pleased to disperse the effects of it over all the Members of his mystick body, that they may more easily assist one another, by the communication of their reciprocal help and advantages. In this association so wisely contrived, of which his most precious blood is the beginning, and the union of hearts the whole strength, his intention was to induce the tenderness of the Eternal Father to grant his mercy to us, by presenting to Him the invaluable price of the blood of his Son, the merits of the Saints, and the power of their suffrages, as the most effectual motives to determine him.

We invite you then to drink of this overflowing stream of indulgence, to enrich yourselves in the inexhaustible treasures of the Church; and, according to the custom and institution of our ancestors, by the consent of our venerable Brethren the Cardinals, &c.

O all of you, then, who are the Children of the Church, do not let flip the prefent occafion, this favourable time, thefe falutary days, of employing them to appeafe the juftice of God, and obtain your pardon! Do not bring, as an excufe for your delay, the fatigues of the voyage, the troubles of the journey.—When we propofe to fhower upon you the gifts of heavenly Grace, to introduce you into the Tabernacles of the Lord, is it proper for you to fuffer yourfelves to be difmayed by inconveniencies, or obftacles, which never deter thofe whom curiofity or the thirft of gain daily lead to the moft diftant regions? Even thofe toils which might difmay you, being undertaken from fo noble a motive, will affift you infinitely in reaping the moft abundant fruits from your penitence. For this reafon, the Church has always looked upon the old cuftom of Pilgrimages as fingularly ufeful; being perfuaded, that the difagreeable inconveniencies which neceffarily attend them, are fo many compenfations for paft fins, and convincing proofs of fincere repentance. If the activity of your

your zeal, the ardour of your love for God, should kindle to such a degree as to make you forget your fatigues, or even to lessen them, be not alarmed; for that holy joy will accelerate your reconciliation, and make a principal part of the satisfaction for those sins that you were charged with, *since much will be forgiven him who hath much loved.*

Hasten then to the City of Sion; come and fill yourselves with the abundance which reigns in the house of the Lord: Every thing here will lead you to repentance; even the aspect of this City, the ordinary habitation of Faith and Piety, the sepulchre of the Apostles, the tomb of the Martyrs. When you see this land which was sprinkled with their blood, when the numberless vestiges of their sanctity present themselves to you on every side, it will be impossible for you to resist that severe repentance which will press upon you, for having withdrawn from the rules and laws which they followed, and which you promised to follow. You will find in the dignity of the Divine worship, in the majesty of the Temples, a powerful voice which will remind you that you are the Temple of the Living God; that he will animate you to adorn it, and with the greater zeal, for your having formerly had an inclination to profane it, and to grieve the Holy Spirit. What muft fupport your refolution, will be the groans and tears of a great number of Chriftians, whom you will behold lamenting their errors, and foliciting their pardon with God. The fentiments of forrow and piety, which you will witnefs, fhall very foon pafs into your hearts with a quicknefs which muft furprife you.

But to this holy forrow, this religious mourning, the moft tender confolations will not fail to fucceed, when you fee a multitude of people and nations haftening in crouds to practife works of juftice and repentance. Can you then ever hope for a more agreeable, a more ravifhing fpectacle, than that of giving to the whole world a fenfible image of the glorious triumph of the Crofs, and of Religion? At leaft, on our part, we fhall be happy on occafion of the almoft univerfal re-union of the Children

dren of the Church; perſuaded that we ſhall find for ourſelves, in the mutual efforts of your charity and piety, an ample ſuperabundance of help and reſources: for we have the fulleſt confidence, that when you ſhall have ſupplicated with us the Divine Diſtributor of Grace for the preſervation of the Faith, for the return of thoſe people who have ſeparated from us, for the tranquillity of the Church, and the happineſs of the Chriſtian Princes, you will before your God remember your common Father, who heartily loves you; and procure, by your vows and intreaties, the ſtrength neceſſary for our weakneſs, to ſupport the immenſe load which has been impoſed upon us.

And you, our venerable Brethren, Patriarchs, Primates, Archbiſhops, and Biſhops, join in our ſollicitude; charge yourſelves with our duties and your own; proclaim to the people who are entruſted to you theſe times of penitence and propitiation; on this occaſion ſo favourable for obtaining the remiſſion of ſins, which our paternal love has preſented to the whole Chriſtian

tian world, in conformity to the ancient practice of the Church, exert your utmost care and authority to produce good fruit for the falvation of fouls. May they hear you explain fuch works of humility and Chriftian charity as they ought to practife, that they may be better difpofed to received the fruits of the Heavenly Grace which is offered to their wants! May they learn, both by your precepts and example, that they ought to have recourfe to faftings, prayer, and alms-giving.

If there be any among you, our venerable Brethren, who will take upon them, as an increafe of their Paftoral labours, the care of conducting in perfon a part of their flock towards the City, which is the Citadel of Religion, and from whence the fources of indulgence fpring, they may be affured that we will receive them with all the fenfibility of the moft tender father. Independently of the luftre which they will procure to our folemnity, they will be enabled, after fuch noble fatigues, after fuch meritorious labours, to reap the moft ample harveft of the gifts of Divine mercy;
and

and at their return with the reſt of their flock, they will have the conſolation of diſtributing to them this precious ſtore.

We do not doubt that our moſt dear Sons, the Emperor, the Kings, and all the Chriſtian Princes, will aſſiſt us with their authority in the vows which we make for the ſalvation of ſouls, ſo that they may have the happy ſucceſs which we expect. We exhort them, therefore, with all our ſoul, to concur with us in ſuch a manner as may correſpond with their love of Religion, and the zeal of our venerable Brethren the Biſhops; to favour their undertaking, and to procure ſafety and convenience on the roads to all Pilgrims. They cannot but know, that ſuch cares muſt contribute greatly to the tranquillity of their reign; and that God will be the more propitious and favourable to them, the more they ſhow themſelves attentive to increaſe his glory for the good of the People.

But in the end, that theſe Preſents may come, &c.

Given at ROME, at St. MARIE-MAJOR, &c. in the Year of our LORD, 1774, the 12th of May, and the fifth Year of our Pontificate.

THIS Bull, with which we finish our collection, may be looked upon as the Testament of Clement XIV. Death, which from that time was ready to feife him, gave him an inward warning that his end was approaching, that this was the laft time he fhould fpeak to the Faithful, and that God required the facrifice of his life.

Every one fhared in this misfortune; and all Communions, however differing in their perfuafions, united in praying to the Lord for the prefervation of a Pontiff, who was fo agreeable to all the crowned heads, and beloved by the whole world. Some recollected the goodnefs with which he had received them; others, his love of wifdom and peace; while he himfelf, regardlefs of the fevere pains which he endured, employed his interrupted refpiration in fight of Heaven for the obtaining the kingdom of truth and concord upon Earth, and to leave after him fome veftiges of his love for peace and juftice.

I was defirous to procure fome of the Letters he wrote during the fix laft months of his life, which was a time of tryal

tryal and pain, but could not poſſibly obtain them. However we have enough to ſhow us, that this great Pontiff adhered eſſentially to the fundamentals of Religion, without being attached to any opinion, and without having the leaſt ſpirit of Party. What is certain, is, that nothing but Prejudice can with-hold his praiſe—Poſterity muſt value him according to his merit, and ſincerely lament their not having known him. Neither paſſion, cabals, nor prejudice, will be capable of obſcuring his glory—and Truth alone will preſent his picture.

F I N I S.

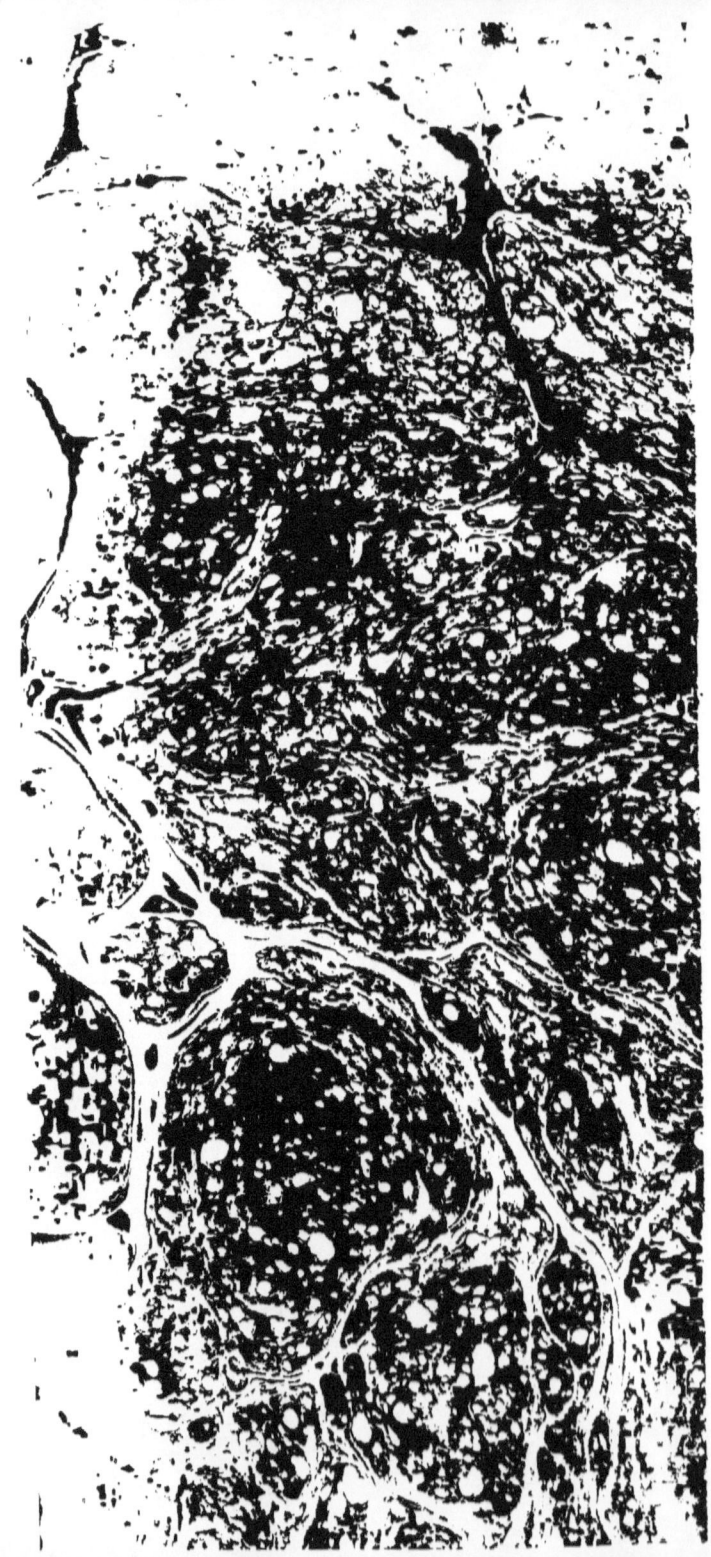

BX   Clemens XIV, pope
1357   Interesting letters of
A4   Pope Clement XIV   5th ed.
1781
v.2

**PLEASE DO NOT REMOVE
CARDS OR SLIPS FROM THIS POCKET**

UNIVERSITY OF TORONTO LIBRARY

www.ingramcontent.com/pod-product-compliance
Lightning Source LLC
Chambersburg PA
CBHW022052230426
43672CB00008B/1149